Common Law & Natural Rights

Common Law & Natural Rights

The Question of Conservative Foundations

Ruben Alvarado

WordBridge

PUBLISHING

Aalten ✤ the Netherlands

www.wordbridge.net

Table of Contents

Foreword

This book began as a revision of *Common-Law Conservatism*, published in 2007. I originally wished to update the argument of that book in the light of the events, both political and economic, of 2008 and early 2009. As it turned out, I wrote something nearly entirely new. To be sure, there are echoes of *Common-Law Conservatism* to be found here and there, and there are paragraphs which have been left virtually unchanged. But in essence this is an entirely new book, with a central argument focusing on the overarching issue at hand as I see it, rather than a plethora of separate issues. That overarching issue is the rule of law – are we to remain a nation ruled by laws, or are we to succumb to rule by men? Are we to be ruled by law, or by will, be it ever so popular? Indeed, the recovery of the rule of law is the goal of this book, and I believe conservative political philosophy more than ever needs to understand this goal. Such is conservatism's birthright, for conservatism stands for law over the popular will, or it stands for nothing.

Aalten, July 4th, 2009
R.C.A.

1. Introduction

Fifty-four years ago, a young man by the name of Russell Kirk published a book that shook the literary, academic, and political world, not so much for its radical ideas as for its lack of them, and beyond that, for its reassertion of a claim to intellectual standing for a set of ideas known precisely for their *rejection* of the radical and revolutionary. For a long time conservatism – that set of ideas of which he wrote – had been in abeyance, if not politically, at least intellectually. That being the case, the outward had come to conform to the inward; without intellectual underpinnings, conservative politics was losing its voice, being all but eliminated from the institutions of public life. In the midst of that decline – Kirk himself labeled it a 150-year-long rout[1] – the young author recaptured the vision of a moral order rooted in tradition, in usage, in historical development, and beyond that, having a basis somehow not in the things of Earth but in those of Heaven. Such ideas, "as startling as they were antique,"[2] caught the liberal intelligentsia by surprise. "The dangerous thing about this particular book was its relative lucidity: conceivably some readers might understand it; and at that prospect, there shivered the people whom Gordon Chalmers, in those years, called the 'disintegrated liberals.'"[3]

Its message reignited a political movement. Since then, conservatism has grown from a fledgling, disparate

---

[1]Kirk, *The Conservative Mind*, p. 5.
[2]Kirk, *The Conservative Mind*, p. iii.
[3]Kirk, *The Conservative Mind*, p. iii.

association of somewhat like-minded citizens into a powerful presence on the political and media scene. But Kirk's
original vision did not gain a similar foothold. To be sure,
conservatism nowadays, at least for the vast majority of
those who claim the title, rests on notions of individual
liberty, self-reliance, limited government, and belief in
God. Kirk, however, went further: in the footsteps of
Edmund Burke, whom he (rightly) considered to be the
founder of the modern conservative movement, he championed the notion of a social order for which "custom,
convention, constitution, and prescription" are the
sources.[4] And for him this was no throwaway phrase. Echoes of a "prescriptive constitution," thus a constitution
based in historical development rather than rational
construction, run throughout the book. Its central theme is
Burke's *critique of natural-rights philosophy;* this latter, said
Kirk echoing Burke, lay at the heart of the radical, revolutionary movements beginning with the French Revolution.[5]

    Such is not the vision of many a contemporary con-
servative. Rather, for him (or her) what seems to predomi-
nate is a common allegiance to the country's founding
documents, namely the Declaration of Independence and
the US Constitution, both of which hail from the era of
Enlightenment and the heyday of natural-rights philosophy. The Declaration's insistence ("We hold these truths
to be self-evident") that "all men are created equal, that
they are endowed by their Creator with certain unalienable
Rights, that among these are Life, Liberty and the pursuit
of Happiness" is the cornerstone, and it is where conservatives hang their hats when it comes to key issues such as

---

[4]Kirk, *The Conservative Mind*, p. iii.

[5]For a flavor of Burke's critique of natural rights, consult the
appendix, wherein excerpts of that critique, as conducted in the
Reflections on the Revolution in France, are contained.

rights to life, liberty, and property. For it is in order "to secure these rights" that "Governments are instituted among Men, deriving their just powers from the consent of the governed, That whenever any Form of Government becomes destructive of these ends, it is the Right of the People to alter or to abolish it, and to institute new Government, laying its foundation on such principles and organizing its powers in such form, as to them shall seem most likely to effect their Safety and Happiness." The Declaration, then, is the American Magna Carta, the creed of limited government and self-reliance, the bastion to which conservatives resort in times of political conflict and culture war.

For its part, the US Constitution contains no such winged language; in fact, it contains no philosophical language at all. Its preamble, while majestic in its way, contains no statement of principle beyond that of an implied popular sovereignty. Some have seen in this a contradiction with the Declaration, for the one speaks of first principles, the other knows nothing of them. Although they are sometimes referred to as components of America's "organic law," even so only the Constitution has undisputed binding legal force. What is evident is that the Constitution was and is considered to be the extension of the Declaration; it is the instrument through which the Declaration's principles were implemented. This is especially true with regard to the separation of powers provided for in the Constitution, as will be explored in detail. And regardless of the Declaration's formal legal status, its moral weight is indisputable; it is its echoes that made Lincoln's Gettysburg Address into the second most famous American political statement: "Four score and seven years ago our fathers brought forth on this continent a new nation, conceived in Liberty, and dedicated to the proposition that all men are created equal."

The conservative resort to Declaration and Constitution is evidenced most recently in conservative commentator Mark Levin's book, *Liberty and Tyranny*,[6] which attained spectacular success upon publication in the spring of 2009, as the full import of the Obama administration and Democrat-led Congress began to be felt and understood among the electorate, and, especially, the conservative element thereof. Levin's book, as another leading conservative commentator, Rush Limbaugh, noted, was "the one-stop shop" summarizing the conservative position, the book which best served to summarize conservatism for friend and foe in an era of liberal expansion of government. Levin claims to be a disciple of Burke, and undoubtedly he echoes many of Burke's concerns regarding the danger of atheistic, rampaging government. Still, he does not explore Burke's notion of a prescriptive constitution, nor Burke's critique of natural rights, which of course stands at the heart of the *Reflections*. For Levin, as for most conservatives, the situation is quite the opposite: natural rights are the guarantee of government restraint.

Building upon the natural-rights basis of the Declaration, Levin, like most other modern conservatives, resorts to that other talisman, the US Constitution, revered for its supposed capacity to keep expansionist government at bay. And likewise, it is not subjected to any criticism. Its major claim to reverence is its institutionalization of the separation of powers, in order to restrict government expansionism. In this, the powers of government are separated and lodged in various independent branches – legislative, executive, and judicial. But the question is not raised

---

[6]Mark Levin, *Liberty and Tyranny: A Conservative Manifesto* (New York: Simon and Schuster, 2009). As of June 19th, it had occupied the no. 1 position on the *New York Times'* bestseller list for hardback books for 12 weeks running – in fact, since its debut.

as to whether the separation of powers itself might not have turned out to have been an ineffective solution to a problem created by the natural-rights basis; that, in fact, it is a gambit which did not pay off, a gambit which, when all is said and done, has actually played into the hands of the statist.

Where does this leave Kirk's "conservative mind"? In a decided quandary: for he spends a good deal of time explaining the American Revolution, not in terms of the natural rights which so prominently accompanied its emergence, but in terms of the prescriptive rights of Englishmen, to which the colonists were entitled, but of which they were being deprived. "Burke disavowed a great part of the principles of Locke, the official philosopher of Whiggism. The theories of Locke were inherited by such diverse legatees as Rousseau in Geneva, Price in the Old Jewry, Fox in St. Stephen's, Bentham in his library, and Jefferson at Monticello; but from among the general ideas of that philosopher, conservatism after Burke retained almost nothing but Locke's contention that government originates out of the necessity for protecting property."[7] And: "By and large, the American Revolution was not an innovating upheaval, but a conservative restoration of colonial prerogatives. Accustomed from their beginnings to self-government, the colonials felt that by inheritance they possessed the rights of Englishmen and by prescription certain rights peculiar to themselves. When a designing king and distant parliament presumed to extend over America powers of taxation and administration never before exercised, the colonies rose to vindicate their prescriptive freedom...."[8] Kirk's conservatism here conflicts profoundly with the conservatism of the vast majority com-

---

[7] Kirk, *The Conservative Mind*, p. 27.
[8] Kirk, *The Conservative Mind*, p. 72.

prising the movement which he helped initiate.

In this, conservatives' dedication to liberty under law remains unquestioned. What is to be questioned is precisely the rationale. Is the Enlightenment notion of natural rights, as enshrined in these statements, truly the only sound basis for securing the liberty conservatives covet? Is it truly the appropriate means to "secure the Blessings of Liberty to ourselves and our Posterity," as the preamble of the Constitution puts it?

This book will argue that it is not, and in fact it constitutes something of a betrayal of the "conservative mind" so eloquently brought back to life by Kirk. In fact, it will argue that the notion of natural rights not only has opened the door to a rampant liberalism, but has closed the door to the only truly sound basis for liberty, to wit, liberty grounded in a preexisting institutional framework, which enables liberty's very existence and which in ineluctable interdependence has grown up together with liberty.

Hence, conservatism's foundations need re-examination precisely in terms of natural rights versus the common law. For a common-law conservatism would understand that liberty is not *just there,* as a pre-existing condition to be preserved by civil government, to which all are entitled simply by virtue of their humanity; much rather, it is a birthright, an heirloom. It is the product of centuries of labor within the context of specifically Western civilization.[9] Nor was its development any sort of blind process; it was the fruit of the deliberate emphasis on establishing a civilization upon fundamental principles both theological and judicial. Western civilization is Christian civilization,

---

[9]"Liberty, Burke knew, had risen through an elaborate and delicate process, and its perpetuation depended upon retaining those habits of thought and action which guided the savage in his slow and weary ascent to the state of civil social man." Kirk, *The Conservative Mind,* p. 21.

but it is also Roman civilization, which explains why "law" could be one of the deciding criteria in its definition. The Western emphasis on law, and specifically on the notion of a "common" law, is what underlies the development of its unique heritage of liberty. In the inexorable course of history, this common-law tradition now maintains a precarious existence only in the Anglo-Saxon countries, and even there (witness Great Britain's dreary apostasy) it is embattled and endangered.

Conservatives instinctively understand this when they compare America to Europe; it is the common-law tradition which divides the one from the other. Conservatives understand that America stands for something different than what is on display in the rest of the world, especially as that "rest of the world" manifests itself in international organizations such as the United Nations; and that that "something different" needs to be protected and preserved in the face of incessant attacks from a supposedly "progressive" global intelligentsia.

It also underlies the political and cultural struggles currently under way between Right and Left in America. This struggle is not one in which natural rights forms a bulwark against some other philosophy, be it utilitarianism, be it some strain or other of post-modernism. Far from being a bulwark, the philosophy of natural rights is a weak reed at this juncture in history.

This essay, then, picks up where Kirk left off. It too is "a criticism of conservative *thought*,"[10] widely divergent though its scope and method might be. Alasdair MacIntyre once wrote that "Burke theorized shoddily"[11] and in this context the same might be said about Kirk: for he never

---

[10]Kirk, *The Conservative Mind*, p. 5.

[11]*Whose Justice? Which Rationality?* (Notre Dame, IN: University of Notre Dame Press, 1988), p. 8.

quite gets around to defining what he means by "prescription" other than that it pertains to something old, something grown, something with historical roots. How is such to be rescued from the clutches of a base reaction or, even worse, a utilitarianism, which justifies things not on the basis of absolute value but in terms of the interests they serve? This points to the question of the transcendent, which likewise Kirk never really bothers with defining other than referring, in good Anglican fashion perhaps, to vague notions of religiosity. And the role of economics, which for many conservatives serves as a touchstone for determining one's commitment to liberty – Kirk is ambivalent here, defending private property but scolding Burke for seeming "to have ignored economic influences spelling death for the eighteenth-century milieu quite so surely as the *Social Contract* repudiated the eighteenth-century mind."[12] In these areas and perhaps more, I intend with this book, indeed, to pick up where Kirk left off, to answer questions he left unanswered, to clear up ambiguities he left behind, to provide conservatism with a defensible intellectual foundation, and more than that, with a platform from which it might successfully take the offensive. And all of this – antiquated though it may sound – in the spirit of Christian charity.

---

[12]Kirk, *The Conservative Mind*, p. 21.

2. The Broken Machinery

We are accustomed to viewing the Constitution as a document drawn up to restrict the exercise of government power. Federalism, one of the means the Constitution provides to this end, restricts the power of the central government over the constituent states. Another means provided for by the Constitution is the so-called separation of powers. The two taken together (along with the Bill of Rights) constitute, in Levin's pregnant phrase, "the Constitution's firewalls."[13]

These firewalls, Levin argues, have been breached. In the present situation, we are witnessing what many view as government gone wild. There seems to be no restraint on what politicians can do, as long as they can get public opinion on their side. And even that is not always required.

Where is the Constitution in this? Levin argues that it is being ignored, its provisions flouted. The trend began with the New Deal, the significance of which lies "not in any one program, but in its sweeping break from our founding principles and constitutional limitations."[14] The New Deal inaugurated the era of government activism by which the federal government "has become a massive, unaccountable conglomerate: It is the nation's largest creditor, debtor, lender, employer, consumer, contractor,

---

[13]*Liberty and Tyranny*, p. 6.
[14]*Liberty and Tyranny*, p. 7.

grantor, property owner, tenant, insurer, health-care pro-
vider, and pension guarantor."[15]

How did the "Statist" manage to accomplish this?
By speaking "in the tongue of the demagogue, concocting
one pretext and grievance after another to manipulate public perceptions and build popular momentum for the di-
vestiture of liberty and property from its rightful possessors."[16] Thus, by manipulating public opinion. Apparently,
what the people want, they will get, Constitution or no
Constitution. And the statist simply proffers. He is a
proficient profferer, for in this manner he builds his power
base. The most effective — those who proffer the most,
and most effectively make the case that they can deliver —
win. Politicians thus win over the people to the pursuit of
goals which may even be "beyond good and evil," goals at
which as individuals they might never connive. Politicians
feed these expectations, and expertly clothe them with
high-sounding justifications.

But at the same time there is intense discontent with
government and its actual accomplishments. If polls are to
be believed, the actual approval of specific government
actions does not always command a majority. This is true
not only of, e.g., the relatively unpopular war in Iraq, but
also for such matters as comprehensive immigration reform. And the institutions of government which are clos-
est to the political arena (the presidency, Congress) generally enjoy dismal approval ratings, as opposed to, e.g., the
military.

So there is a certain degree of ambivalence in contemporary institutions of popular governance. Is it because
the promises politicians make are not realized? Or is it because the electorate is conflicted, on the one hand desiring

---

[15] *Liberty and Tyranny*, pp. 7-8.
[16] *Liberty and Tyranny*, p. 8.

the things politicians promise, while on the other realizing that something isn't quite right, that whatever is being carried out in the people's name, it is not what the people qua people really want?

This points to a problem in the working of representation. The role that the media plays in mediating the relationship between citizens and their representatives is a crucial element which usually goes unexplored. We rely on the *media* to *mediate,* which means that the media serve as a means to connect citizen with representative. They are, in a very real sense, the custodians of democracy. But who is to be the custodian of the media? *Qui custodes custodiat?* If disinformation is the rule, whereby both politicians and citizens are led by the nose by a media which itself is involved in a game of manipulation, then in the final analysis it is the information providers themselves who hold power in a polity ostensibly ruled by the people.

Yet this dominance of the media is itself not the ultimate explanation, but a by-product of the arrangement. Government has been given unlimited power, as long as that power is utilized to fulfill the wishes of the people. Against this power there is no law. And where such an arrangement is in place, the key is to manipulate public opinion in order to legitimize any and every use of power, constitutional or otherwise. The media simply plays a specific, albeit key, role in this process.

The problem, then, is that the people have been flattered into believing that whatever "the people" as a collective entity, which in practice is a majority, desires, ought to be provided them, and the means ought not be begrudged.

We need to have recourse to expert analysis. The best available, conducted by Nobel prize winner Friedrich

A. Hayek,[17] has been mired in obscurity, for reasons which remain a mystery (perhaps because democracy itself cannot be subjected to criticism?). Hayek's analysis dispels the mists enveloping modern democracy's feet of clay.

"Civilization largely rests on the fact that the individuals have learnt to restrain their desires for particular objects and to submit to generally recognized rules of just conduct. Majorities, however, have not yet been civilized in this manner because they do not have to obey rules."[18] Majorities have been conditioned to believe that whatever they decide upon, that is, whatever their will may be, is law. The understanding of law as something standing over and conditioning sovereignty has been lost. "The belief that all on which a majority can agree is by definition just has for several generations been impressed upon popular opinion." And this leads to the inevitable corollary: "Need we be surprised that in the conviction that what they resolve is necessarily just, the existing representative assemblies have ceased even to consider in the concrete instances whether this is really so?"[19]

Here already we have arrived at the crux of the problem. With sovereignty having been given this absolute, above-the-law air, we get representative bodies charged with carrying out the will of this absolute sovereign. This establishes a vortex of power wherein politicians are encouraged to bid up their promises to carry out the wishes of the sovereign people; politicians who rather point out the limitations of such power fall out of favor.

What is the result in practice? There are few general

---

[17]Friedrich A. Hayek, *Law, Legislation, and Liberty: Volume 3: The Political Order of a Free People* (Chicago: The University of Chicago Press, 1979).

[18]Hayek, *Law, Legislation, and Liberty: Volume 3*, p. 7.

[19]*Ibid.*

"wishes" shared jointly by a majority. What happens in fact is that pressure groups form which lobby each for their particular wish or goal, and form shifting alliances with other pressure groups in order to form a majority in the representative assembly. It is *this* majority, not a majority of voters per se, which determines what actually happens in government. This kind of horse-trading of interests in the name of political expediency, although often viewed as corruption, in fact is the inevitable concomitant of representative government with unlimited power.[20]

This explains the general discontent with government. And yet government continues with the same sorts of policies, *with the continued support of the voters* — voila! the conflicted electorate. "This domination of government by coalitions of organized interests ... is usually regarded by the outsider as an abuse, or even a kind of corruption. It is, however, the inescapable result of a system in which government has unlimited powers to take whatever measures are required to satisfy the wishes of those on whose support it relies. A government with such powers cannot refuse to exercise them and still retain the support of a majority."[21]

So it is not a mere matter of media manipulation; the disconnect between what the people want *in general* and what the people want *as coalitions of pressure groups* is what underlies the general discontent with politics. "The agree-

---

[20]Hayek, *Law, Legislation, and Liberty: Vol. 3*, pp. 8ff.

[21]Hayek, *Law, Legislation, and Liberty: Vol. 3*, p. 15. Hayek continues: "We have no right to blame the politicians for doing what they must do in the position in which we have placed them. We have created conditions in which it is known that the majority has power to give any particular section of the population whatever it demands. But a government that possesses such unlimited powers can stay in office only by satisfying a sufficiently large number of pressure groups to assure itself of the support of a majority."

ment on which such a programme for governmental action is based is something very different from that common opinion of a majority which it was hoped would be the determining force in a democracy.... A series of deals by which the wishes of one group are satisfied in return for the satisfaction of the wishes of another ... may determine aims for common action of a coalition, but does not signify popular approval of the overall results. *The outcome may indeed be wholly contrary to any principles which the several members of the majority would approve if they ever had an opportunity to vote on them.*"[22]

Hayek's conclusion is that only a return to a proper understanding of the rule of law, as something which transcends even the will of the electorate, can save democracy. "The only defence that a politician has against such pressure is to point to an established principle which prevents him from complying and which he cannot alter. No system in which those who direct the use of the resources of government are not bound by unalterable rules can escape becoming an instrument of the organized interests."[23] The electorate has to be reconditioned to accept the concept of the rule of law as binding even upon its own will.

Was not the doctrine of the separation of powers supposed to have accomplished this task of restraint on will by law? For the Founding Fathers realized the danger of uncontrolled legislative power. Their solution was to isolate that power in a separate branch of government, and restrict its powers. James Madison cautioned in *The Federalist*, no. 48: "In a representative republic, where the executive magistracy is carefully limited, both in the extent and the duration of its power; and where the legislative power

---

[22]Hayek, *Law, Legislation, and Liberty: Vol. 3*, p. 15. Emphasis added.

[23]Hayek, *Law, Legislation, and Liberty: Vol. 3*, pp. 16-17.

is exercised by an assembly, which is inspired by a supposed influence over the people, with an intrepid confidence in its own strength; which is sufficiently numerous to feel all the passions which actuate a multitude; yet not so numerous as to be incapable of pursuing the objects of its passions, by means which reason prescribes; it is against the enterprising ambition of this department, that the people ought to indulge all their jealousy, and exhaust all their precautions." Disperse the powers of sovereignty among the three branches of government, in line with the expositions of John Locke and Baron de Montesquieu, so that the executive, the legislative, and the judicial branches might condition each other in the exercise of power, such that none might become predominant.

And yet, as Hayek's analysis so brilliantly demonstrates, the mechanism is not working as it was set up to. "It appears that we have unwittingly created a machinery which makes it possible to claim the sanction of an alleged majority for measures which are in fact not desired by a majority, and which may even be disapproved by a majority of the people; and that this machinery produces an aggregate of measures that not only is not wanted by anybody, but that could not as a whole be approved by any rational mind because it is inherently contradictory."[24]

Why, then, has not the separation of powers, as embodied in the Constitution, not functioned to restrict the exercise of power? Here again, Hayek provides the conclusive analysis. It is because legislatures historically are instruments of government, not of legislation! At least, not of legislation proper. Legislation *proper* has to do with lawmaking, and *law is something other than government.* Law, at bottom, is a general, universally applicable rule of just conduct. Law does not prescribe specific actions, it only de-

---

[24]Hayek, *Law, Legislation, and Liberty: Vol. 3*, p. 6.

limits the spheres within which actions may take place. It is in this sense negative: it does not direct, but only restricts.[25] Government, on the other hand, is the power to pursue particular goals, to carry out particular policies. Stahl, whose analysis anticipates that of Hayek in fundamental ways, grounds the difference partly in the distinction between laws and decrees. "Decrees, being mere acts of government power ... are certainly general rules, just as are laws; yet they are fundamentally distinguished from laws, for laws comprise *legal principles*, while decrees only comprise a leading of common activity to realize *purposes*." Government has the task both of executing the laws which it receives, and of issuing and implementing decrees, which establish policies in pursuit of specific goals. The one is general and enduring, the other is specific and passing. "Accordingly, laws are usually lasting, decrees more varying. For duration corresponds to the inner necessity, to the character of law, while movement corresponds to that ongoing pursuit of the better, the more beneficial, which is the character of government."[26]

The distinction between law and government is an enduring one in Western constitutional history. McIlwain saw it underlying the medieval concept of the state, as expressed in the opposition *gubernaculum-jurisdictio*, where *gubernaculum* pertained to government action, *jurisdictio* to the negative restriction on government by laws which government is bound to execute.[27] It was *jurisdictio* which, during the conflict between Parliament and monarchy in early

---

[25]Stahl, *Principles of Law*, p. 20.

[26]Stahl, *Die Staatslehre und die Principien des Staatsrechts* [The Doctrine of State and the Principles of State Law], §. 58. A translation of this important work, by the author of the current book, is forthcoming.

[27]Charles Howard McIlwain, *Constitutionalism: Ancient and Modern* (Ithaca, NY: Cornell University Press, 1947).

17th-century England, the common lawyers, headed by Sir Edward Coke, championed over against the royal prerogative, *gubernaculum,* the primacy of which was asserted by James I and Charles I. Coke argued in favor of the supremacy of the common law against both king and Parliament.[28]

It is this understanding of the primacy of law over government which has been lost, and it has been lost in the transition from monarchy to government based on the will of the people. What the Stuart kings could not accomplish – the primacy of government by prerogative – representative government has.

This was not the intention of the champions of popular sovereignty, at least not until Jean-Jacques Rousseau came along with his notion of the General Will as the expression of law. But there was definitely a complacency regarding popular government which led one to believe that it would be enough to establish a popularly-elected legislature to oversee the affairs of government, and to restrict the government proper to an executive function, whereby government simply executed the laws promulgated by the legislature.

What this orientation did not take sufficiently into account is the need to restrict the legislature precisely to its assigned task of legislation. As we shall see, it did nothing of the kind, and in fact could not have, for the historical role of these "legislatures" was not in fact legislation, but government.

This complacency can be followed in the work of John Locke, one of the originators of the separation of powers doctrine. Locke was well aware of the danger in-

---

[28]At least sometimes: see R. A. MacKay, "Coke: Parliamentary Sovereignty or the Supremacy of the Law?" In *Michigan Law Review,* Vol. 22, No. 3 (Jan., 1924), pp. 215-247.

herent in a lawmaking power. To hinder this, he argued that the legislative branch should be restricted to making laws, thus rules meeting the criteria of law proper: "The legislative or supreme authority cannot assume to itself a power to rule, by extemporary, arbitrary decrees; but is bound to dispense justice, and to decide the rights of the subject, by promulgated, standing laws, and known authorised judges" (§. 136).

> Whatever form the commonwealth is under, the ruling power ought to govern by declared and received laws, and not by extemporary dictates and undetermined resolutions.... For all the power the government has, being only for the good of the society, as it ought not to be arbitrary and at pleasure, so it ought to be exercised by established and promulgated laws; that both the people may know their duty, and be safe and secure within the limits of the law; and the rulers too kept within their bounds, and not be tempted, by the power they have in their hands, to employ it to such purposes, and by such measures, as they would not have known, and own not willingly (§. 137).

And yet, Locke so constitutes the legislative body that it stands supreme even over the law, and nothing but what it approves can have the force of law (§. 134):

> This legislative is not only the supreme power of the commonwealth, but sacred and unalterable in the hands where the community have once placed it; nor can any edict of any body else, in what form soever conceived, or by what power soever backed, have the force and obligation of a law, which has not its sanction from that legislative which the public has chosen and appointed; for

without this the law could not have that, which is
absolutely necessary to its being a law, the consent
of the society; over whom nobody can have a
power to make laws, but by their own consent,
and by authority received from them.

In order to place some restriction on this power of
the legislature, Locke argued for the need to remove from
it the capacity to execute the laws it makes. The executive,
then, functions as government proper, with a continuing
existence and activity; the legislature, on the other hand,
having no need of an ongoing presence, only comes together periodically to establish laws, which thereafter lead
a continuing existence; and the legislators themselves disperse, to live under the very laws they have made (§. 143).
"Because the laws, that are at once, and in a short time
made, have a constant and lasting force, and need a perpetual execution, or an attendance thereunto: therefore it is
necessary there should be a power always in being, which
should see to the execution of the laws that are made, and
remain in force. And thus the legislative and executive
power come often to be separated" (§. 144).

Locke thus put forward two means to ensure that
government is kept under restraint: the empowerment of
the legislature only to make law, as opposed to issuing decrees, and the separation of the executive from the legislature, so that the same persons do not both make the law
and execute it; "because it may be too great a temptation
to human frailty, apt to grasp at power, for the same persons, who have the power of making laws, to have also in
their hands the power to execute them; whereby they may
exempt themselves from obedience to the laws they make,
and suit the law, both in its making and execution, to their
own private advantage, and thereby come to have a distinct interest from the rest of the community, contrary to
the end of society and government" (§. 143).

The problem here is that Locke evinces no understanding of the difference between law and government,
between *gubernaculum* and *jurisdictio*, and simply asserts a
legislative power restricted to the promulgation of law
proper – an assertion which should rather have come not
as an assertion at all, but as a result laboriously derived and
conclusively developed: for such a thing did not exist then,
and has not gained much of an existence since.

Stahl already argued the insufficiency of the solution, in pointing out that the separation of powers dena-
tures government proper by transforming government into
a mere executive of laws. This may sound like a restriction,
but in actuality it is a release from restriction. "[The separation of powers doctrine]… overlooks the actual, free
governing power, and assimilates it to the executive power,
i.e., the mere execution of given laws. In the current praxis
of constitutional states, this has the disadvantageous consequence that one views every standing order not issued in
consequence of a preceding law, thus not mere execution,
as for example a school ordinance, itself as a law…. The
state then appears as a great law machine, and each part of
the entire mechanism meshes with each other so as to
make laws and apply those that are made. There are then
decrees either for the laws or against them, but none
which are by any means independent within the laws."[29]
Law and decree, legislation and government, become en-
tangled in each other; law loses its function as a restriction
on government power, and in fact loses its specific content.

> The executive power, entirely divested of the leg-
> islative, ceases to be a power and becomes the
> mere tool of the latter. The consistent implemen-

---

[29]Stahl, *Die Staatslehre*, §. 59.

tation of the doctrine of separation therefore frustrates the original intention to secure the position of the citizen between two opposing independent powers. What it achieves is entirely the same as what Rousseau, the declared opponent of the doctrine of division, wanted. For he no less demands the division, in that the subject of execution *(Gouvernement)* and that of legislation *(Souverain)* are to be separate, only he does not wish the former to be a power. The factual result finally is then the simple conversion of monarchy into democracy.[30]

Far from becoming the executive of the law, government absorbs the law. Law and government become indistinguishably one.

Hayek ruthlessly exposes the situation in entire clarity. Locke's strictures, whereby the legislative power was to be restricted to law proper, were laudable, but fantasy. For the legislature never was a legislature in the strict sense of the word, but a body which arose out of the need to oversee and eventually assume control of the government, through the mechanism of taxation and representation. This development – however laudable in itself – should never have been confused with a separation of powers in the sense put forward by Locke and Montesquieu. Legislatures historically have been extensions of government; true legislation has been an afterthought, when not pursued in direct opposition to law proper.

If we are not to be misled by the word 'legislature', therefore, we shall have to remember that it is no more than a sort of courtesy title conferred on assemblies which had primarily arisen as in-

---

[30]*Ibid.*

struments of representative *government*. Modern
legislatures clearly derive from bodies which existed before the deliberate making of rules of just
conduct was even considered possible, and the
latter task was only later entrusted to institutions
habitually concerned with very different tasks. The
noun 'legislature' does not in fact appear before
the middle of the seventeenth century and it
seems doubtful whether it was then applied to the
existing 'constituted bodies' (to use R.A. [*sic*]
Palmer's useful term) as a result of a dimly perceived conception of a separation of powers, or,
rather, in a futile attempt to restrict bodies claiming control over government to the making of
general laws. However that may be, they were in
fact never so confined, and 'legislature' has become simply a name for representative assemblies
occupied chiefly with directing or controlling government.[31]

Were the US Founding Fathers able to construct a
system averting this state of affairs? In other words, were
they aware of the legislation/government distinction, and
did they take pains to implement that understanding in the
federal government? Hayek answers in the negative.
Through the separation of legislative, executive, and judicial branches, the Founders had hoped to subject both
government and individuals to the rule of law. "They
could hardly have foreseen that, because the legislature
was also entrusted with the direction of government, the
task of stating rules of just conduct and the task of direct-

---

[31] Hayek, *Law, Legislation, and Liberty: Volume 1: Rules and Order*
(Chicago: The University of Chicago Press, 1973), p. 129. The
Palmer reference is to Robert R. Palmer, *The Age of the Democratic
Revolution: Volume I: The Challenge* (Princeton: Princeton University
Press, 1959).

ing particular activities of government to specific ends would come to be hopelessly confounded, and that law would cease to mean only such universal and uniform rules of just conduct as would limit all arbitrary coercion." Hence, their aim was confounded, and they never quite attained the goal of a separation of powers. "Instead they produced in the USA a system under which, often to the detriment of the efficiency of government, the power of organizing and directing government was divided between the chief executive and a representative assembly elected at different times and on different principles and therefore frequently at loggerheads with each other."[32]

Yet this is not the whole story. What the Founders did accomplish – more specifically, what the Federalists managed to establish in the teeth of Jeffersonian Republican opposition – was the institution of judicial review by which the judiciary, preeminently the Supreme Court, was empowered to pass judgement on legislation and government decrees, in the name not only of the written Constitution but also of the entire received body of law.

Dietze has described the disparate nature of this body of law, aptly characterizing it as "older law:" "It ranged from the principles of the common law to those of natural law and the law of God; from such general maxims as the social contract and free government to those of natural rights and natural justice." Faced with this multifariousness, judicial review became much more than the mere examination of laws in the light of the text of the written constitution. "Naturally, this great variety of values was not likely to create a precise and clearly defined concept of the older law, and this was not altered by the fact that some of these values were put down in so many words in

---

[32]Hayek, *Law, Legislation, and Liberty: Vol. 3*, pp. 105-106.

famous documents, such as the colonial charters and the Declaration of Independence. Since, in turn, the older law was in various ways intertwined with the written Constitution, that Constitution was by no means that clearly defined document which corresponded to the ideal of a Thomas Paine. Consequently the body of constitutional law could not possibly become too concise either."[33] It took a mighty effort on the part of judges imbued with the common-law spirit of law formation to make sense of this confusion, and fashion a legal system answering to the principles of the common law.

> It is obvious that such a vague and mystical concept of a Constitution cannot fulfill one essential purpose of the law, namely, legal security. Therefore, it was necessary to concretize the manifestations of the older law. Naturally, this task fell to those whose "proper and peculiar province" is to interpret the laws, the judges (Hamilton, *Federalist* no. 78). By applying the law to the case before them, they moulded what was nothing but a mass of constitutional and extra-constitutional principles into a specific Constitution. And whereas their interpretation of the law would take into account the specific conditions of a specific time and thus be very much down to earth, it would always be remindful of the values of the older law, and thus be close to the Heavens. The judges performed their task so admirably that American government came to be characterized as a "government of laws – not of men," a term which symbolizes the transmutation of the older law into concrete norms, emphasizing, at the same time, the superiority of the former over the latter.

---

[33]Gottfried Dietze, "Judicial Review in Europe and America," in *Virginia Law Review* Vol. 44, No. 8 (Dec., 1958), p. 1245.

Like the sculptor who, when moulding his clay into a piece of art, is guided by considerations of aesthetics, the American judges were, when forming the law into legal decisions through an interpretation of the Constitution, guided by considerations of an ethical justice.[34]

Hence Dietze argues that "the American Constitution did by no means, as Thomas Paine thought, owe its existence to a mere constituent act by the American people. Rather, it was largely declaratory of norms that had — though unwritten — been accepted throughout the colonial period."[35] Nevertheless, as is clear from the description he provides of "older law," there was not as yet any clear understanding of the disparity between the philosophy of natural rights and that of the common law. These continued in uneasy harness together. Why this situation was untenable will be explored in the following chapter.

---

[34]Dietze, "Judicial Review in Europe and America," pp. 1245-1246.

[35]Dietze, "Judicial Review in Europe and America," p. 1247.

3. The Natural-Rights Basis

The doctrine of the separation of powers was intended to bridle government, but it left out the main instrument for bridling government, the establishment of an opposition between government and law. Why did its exponents take this approach? They were quite aware of the danger to liberty formed by unaccountable government. But their focus had been on the restraint of government wherein the executive and the legislative powers were joined, absolute monarchy being the most glaring example. Their views of legislative power as a separate branch of government were much more sanguine, which is why they could repose in a solution wherein the legislative and executive powers were delimited and separated.

This complacency can only be explained by a changed view of law. Law was losing its sanctity; it was being seen as subject to modification, if not wholesale re-creation. This way of thinking with regard to law began in earnest with the French political philosopher Jean Bodin (✝1596), who posited a new view of sovereignty, whereby the relationship of sovereignty to law was transformed, from one in which the sovereign discovered or recognized or sanctioned the law to one in which the sovereign asserted or created the law. Bodin put forward this novel doctrine as a solution to the wars of religion ravaging his native France, which had the disputing parties asserting the primacy of fundamental law or an ancient constitution as a justification for revolt. By redefining sovereignty precisely as the source of law, Bodin placed the sovereign above any such dispute, thus restoring peace.

This fervent desire for peace and the recovery of concord characterized the late 16th and early 17th centuries.[36] It was also shared by Hugo Grotius, the Dutch Arminian who himself fell victim to civil war in his home country, the Dutch Republic, from which he was exiled. Grotius had been a member of the ruling regent class in Holland, and, as a leading apologist for their regime, had argued that the States of Holland, which were manned by this regent class, were the absolute possessors of sovereignty. They were thus beholden neither to the people nor to the prince (this would be the *stadhouder*, the Prince of Orange) in their exercise of this sovereignty.

Grotius based his argument on the notion of an ancient constitution, by which the States of Holland from ancient times had been in possession of sovereignty. But when opposition to their rule grew into a formidable force, under the leadership of Maurice, Prince of Orange, and the vast majority of the Reformed church establishment, the leaders of the States party, among whom was Grotius, were incarcerated or banished, and the major figure among them, Johan van Oldenbarnevelt, was executed for high treason.

Having this experience behind him, Grotius could no longer call upon the ancient constitution argument, which was effective against the foreign domination of Spain, but not against home-grown opposition. So he forged a new synthesis as a basis for law and state, making use of the received materials at hand from political and

---

[36]This is a recurrent theme in the fine book by Richard Tuck, *Philosophy and Government 1572-1651* (Cambridge: Cambridge University Press, 1993), which provides useful background to the discussion here.

legal philosophy. Grotius was the first to base political obligation on *natural rights*.

To understand the significance of this, one must come to grips with an essential concept of legal philosophy, to wit, subjective right. By this concept, which was laboriously developed in, and only in, the Western legal tradition, the individual was recognized to have a power of assertion and activity which could serve as the basis for specific legal relations. In other words, the individual as individual was recognized in law as a primordial entity not to be ignored; in fact, he was an essential building block, which had to be taken into account in the formation of law.

Stahl's explanation of subjective right is the best available. This "law in the subjective sense," thus subjective right, "is the *ethical power* which a man has over against others in the sphere allotted to him by the legal order, by virtue of that order. Its essence is not merely the negative of allowance or the intransitive [i.e., lacking an object] of freedom, but the positive and transitive of ethical power against others."[37] It is the legal reflection of personality, within the structure of the legal order. "Law in the subjective sense, e.g., the right of men due him in all his life positions, constructs, in that it is his own power inhering in him, a true center about which the entire external world (things, actions of others, etc.) is related as controlled object, and in accordance with which the content of legal norms is often determined."

Even so, this keystone of the legal order is secondary, not primary. In other words, the law is more than rights, and the formation of law is more than that which this power of subjective right can accomplish. "[Subjective right] is ... a *secondary principle of the legal order* alongside the

---

[37]Stahl, *Principles of Law,* p. 97.

primary and absolute principle: the *purpose* (τέλος) of *life relations*. As secondary principle, however, it is always based upon this latter. Its own content and range is originally and essentially derived from, and the coherence of all the rights of all men lies in, this objective higher principle."[38]

Subjective right was developed as a secondary principle of the legal order. Grotius was the first to invert the order: he made subjective right into the primary, originating principle of the legal order. In fact, his innovation was nothing less than to harness the concept of subjective right so as to attribute to the individual the very same principle of sovereignty that Bodin had developed for the state. Just as, for Bodin, sovereignty was the source of law, for Grotius subjective right was the source of law, restricted, in the same way as was Bodinian sovereignty, only by divine and natural law. *Grotius simply transferred the character of Bodinian sovereignty to subjective right.*

This becomes especially clear in the manner in which Grotius derives the power of the sword wielded by the state. It comes from the individuals who have formed it! "Is not the power to punish essentially a power that pertains to the state? Not at all! On the contrary, just as every right of the magistrate comes to him from the state, so has the same right come to the state from private individuals ... Therefore, since no one is able to transfer a thing that he never possessed, it is evident that the right of chastisement was held by private persons before it was held by the state."[39] As Tuck notes, this is precisely the doctrine John

---

[38]Stahl, *Principles of Law,* pp. 98-99.

[39]Grotius, *De Jure Praedae Commentarius,* I, trans. G.L. Williams (Oxford, 1950), pp. 91-2; quoted in Richard Tuck, *Natural Rights Theories: Their Origin and Development* (Cambridge: Cambridge University Press, 1979), p. 62. See also in this connection Brian Tierney, *The Idea of Natural Rights: Studies on Natural Rights, Natural Law, and Church Law, 1150-1625* (Grand Rapids, MI: Wm. B. Eerdmans Publishing Co.,

Locke presented to the world in his *Second Treatise* as a
"very strange doctrine" (§. 9). Locke could not have
known of Grotius' statement here, since the manuscript in
which it was contained was not published until the 19th
century. But Grotius' entire system, as published in the
ground-breaking *Law of War and Peace* (1625), entailed this
understanding, and it only took Locke to draw the appropriate conclusions.

The sovereign individual, then, is the source of the
sovereign state; the sovereign state is the source of law,
because the sovereign individual is.

Law is the product of the sovereign individual. This
is the significance of the doctrine of natural rights. The
actual content that is poured into this vessel – whether the
Lockean trinity of life, liberty, and property, or the
modified Jeffersonian version of life, liberty, and the pursuit of happiness, or the modern bloated version including
rights to work, leisure, vacation time, not to mention "pri-
vacy" – is secondary. For they are not what is essential to
the doctrine.

Natural rights are supposed to restrict government.
But ultimately they only serve to justify legislative cum
governmental supremacy. To claim a restriction in the legislative power by virtue of a right to life, or a right to property, is to return to a condition where subjective right is
secondary, and an objective legal order is primary. For
rights are only an expression of the power which is subjective right; that power always stands over its expressions,
and so the power of subjective right always stands over the
various rights it expresses. Hence, the essence of an im-
puted primacy of subjective right is precisely the removal
of any restriction on lawmaking power! Law is what these
sovereign individuals make of it, individually, and, by mu-

2001 [1997]), pp. 333f.

tual agreement, collectively.

Therefore Grotius' definition of sovereignty – "That is called Supreme, whose Acts are not subject to another's Power, so that they cannot be made void by any other human Will"[40] – echoes Bodin's. Likewise with Locke's definition of the legislative power – "the supreme power of the commonwealth," which is "sacred and unalterable in the hands where the community have once placed it," regarding which no "edict of any body else, in what form soever conceived, or by what power soever backed, have the force and obligation of a law, which has not its sanction from that legislative which the public has chosen and appointed" (*Second Treatise*, §. 134). Apart from this legislative power, vested in an assembly by the sovereign individuals who have come together to form a government, there is no law.

This is a far cry from the received tradition of *jurisdictio* as a co-equal power conditioning and limiting *gubernaculum*. In fact, it is a recipe for the complete inhalation of *jurisdictio* by *gubernaculum*, of law by government. Which is, of course, what has come about.

The separation of powers has thus failed in its stated goal of restricting government power, precisely because, in the enthusiasm for subjective right, it allows of no other power outside of government capable of restricting it. The sovereign individual, when it comes down to it, turns out not only to be an all-conquering power, but to be a weak reed, in view of the fact that he has been coopted into the machine via the mechanics of interest-group politics. An *institutional* break on government power is entirely

---

[40]Hugo Grotius, *The Rights of War and Peace*, Book I, ed. Richard Tuck, trans. Jean Barbeyrac (Indianapolis: Liberty Fund, 2005), p. 259.

lacking.[41]

Berman highlighted this failure of the separation of powers by comparing it to the medieval "two-swords" arrangement, whereby a public church institution effectively countered an overweening state. "Many centuries later," wrote Berman, "the concept of the rule of law came to be identified with the separation of the legislative, administrative, and judicial powers" whereby "power was divided, although in the earlier period the 'checks and balances' had been provided chiefly by concurrent polities within the same territory rather than by concurrent branches of the same polity."[42] Just so; whatever faults the medieval arrangement had, it did provide for a serious check on state power.

But this is not to argue for a restoration of an *imperium in imperio,* such as the Roman church formed in the medieval polity. A public church with that kind of power, capable of intervening in all levels of private as well as public life through an expansive conception of spiritual jurisdiction, is neither necessary nor desirable. What institutional arrangement, then, can meet the need to restrain government?

Berman alludes to a solution when he points out the other main difference between the medieval and modern "separation of powers." In both, "law was derived from, and rooted in, a reality that transcended the existing structure of political power," but with this difference, that "In the later period, that transcendent reality was found in human rights, democratic values, and other related beliefs. In

---

[41]The failure of judicial review within the framework of the separation of powers will be discussed below.

[42]Harold Berman, *Law and Revolution: The Formation of the Western Legal Tradition* (Cambridge, MA: Harvard University Press, 1983), p. 294.

the earlier period it had been found in divine and natural justice."[43] Natural rights, the enthronement of subjective right, form our transcendent reality; but what we need is to recover another transcendent reality, rooted in divine and natural justice, yet concretely expressed in the institutions of positive law: and that would be the common law.

---

[43]*Ibid.*

4. The Common-Law Method

To recover the common law as an institutional framework capable of restraining the state, some basic principles need to be established.

First, the relationship between law and the state. The state may be sovereign, and yet, it is not the source of law. The law is coordinate with the state; the two mutually condition each other. Stahl's exposition, here as well, is the best available.

The state has a dual aspect, Stahl writes, "the *ruling authority* or *state power (imperium)*, i.e., the power exercised by men, and the *law (lex)*." The one is personality, either natural (prince) or artificial (assembly); the other is "an enduring conviction which must undergird the true personal will." Both taken together constitute the personal rule of the state.[44]

But the one cannot be reduced to the other. "Law and state power, then, relate to each other the way in which, in individual persons ... character relates to will (power of decision)." The one is general, enduring, the other is particular, constituted by specific action; state power, or government proper, presupposes and acts in terms of the law. "The law is the ground and presupposition of state power, through which it is state power (laws of form of government, succession to the throne), and it is partly restriction, partly the positive grounds of determina-

---

[44]Stahl, *Die Staatslehre*, §. 53.

tion of the exercise of state power; this latter must not overstep it, and must execute it." But the law likewise is based in and supported by state power, for otherwise it could not maintain an existence: "State power is the ground and presupposition of the law – the law is valid because of the regard of state power, which also has the power to change the law and further to develop it, and, within the law, the state power rules freely in a broad sphere.... Mutual presupposition and interaction exist between law and state power, despite which each has its own independent sphere." Where this understanding is lost, the absolute state arises: "when one views the state power, even if the sovereign people *(volonté générale)*, as the primary thing, this of necessity leads to state absolutism ... the law becomes the product of state power instead of being accepted as just as original an extant power."[45]

This, at bottom, is the understanding that needs to be recovered. But how is it to be recovered? How is it to be implemented?

The best outline of a solution is perhaps that given by Hayek in the three volumes of *Law, Legislation, and Liberty*. In the third volume, devoted specifically to this issue, Hayek, as we have seen, focuses on the problem of the legislature as being an instrument of government rather than legislation. The solution, then, is to create a true legislative body, separate from the current legislatures, concerned as they are with matters of government proper, the "legislation" of which is either not legislation at all or which constitutes intervention in the legal order that violates its inherent structure and integrity. Hayek proposes a legislature along the lines of Locke's original proposal (see p. 17 above), concerned solely with general rules of conduct, rather than particular directives and commands.

---

[45] *Ibid.*

There would then be two elected bodies charged with representing the people, a Legislative Assembly concerned with the law, and a Governmental Assembly concerned with affairs of government, centered in taxation and expenditure. The Legislative Assembly "in general would have the power only in so far as it proved its intention to be just by committing itself to universal rules intended to be applied in an unknown number of future instances and over the application of which to particular cases it had no further power." These rules would be "intended to apply to an indefinite number of unknown future instances, to serve the formation and preservation of an abstract order whose concrete contents were unforeseeable, but not the achievement of particular concrete purposes, and finally to exclude all provisions intended or known to affect principally particular identifiable individuals or groups."[46] The Governmental Assembly would do what legislative assemblies already do, with the exception of legislation proper as here understood. Conflicts between the two would be settled by a specially established Constitutional Court.

Interestingly enough, Hayek does not develop the idea of the existing body of private law, as embodied in the common law, as itself being a restriction on government, it being the embodiment of those "rules regulating the conduct of person towards others, applicable to an unknown number of future instances and containing prohibitions delimiting (but of course not specifying) the boundaries of the protected domain of all persons and organized groups."[47] Volume 1 of *Law, Legislation, and Liberty* had been devoted to the exposition of this legal order precisely in order to delineate it in opposition to the order of gov-

---

[46]Hayek, *Law, Legislation, and Liberty: Vol. 3*, p. 109.
[47]Hayek, *Law, Legislation, and Liberty: Vol. 3*, p. 100.

ernment, with its commands and directives, its particular actions and policies. Hayek took pains to explain the necessity of a court-evolved, adjudicatory approach to the development of this law. Why did he not, in volume 3, adduce the judiciary, the guardian of "nomos," as he calls it, as itself a barrier to government action?

The answer must be that the law has been so corrupted by legislation as now conducted, that the contemporary judiciary offers little relief in the way of a restoration of law proper. In fact, the contemporary judiciary, as a vehicle of judicial activism, is little more than a further development of government intervention and interference in the law. All three branches of government as established by the Constitution are cooperating in the Great Goal of expanding government power.

What is needed is a truly independent judiciary, operating in terms of the received common-law tradition and not simply in terms of statute law, or whatever the legislature palms off as law. Such a judiciary should maintain the integrity of the legal order as a self-contained body of law, coherent in itself. Such a conception of the legal order is a corollary of the adjudicatory process itself. The inner logic of adjudication between independent parties equal before the law requires appeal to the principles of justice standing over all parties, including the judge. The resulting decisions help to shape and develop law proper.[48] Furthermore, the constraints of conflict resolution, based on what the participants in a conflict had reasonably to expect, is an essential element in the formation of law, which legislation must imitate but can never replace.

Hayek succinctly describes this development by way of inner logic by drawing an analogy to the progress of science. "As in all other fields," he writes, "advance is here

---

[48]Hayek, *Law, Legislation, and Liberty: Vol. 1*, pp. 97ff.

achieved by our moving within an existing system of thought and endeavouring by a process of piecemeal tinkering, or 'immanent criticism', to make the whole more consistent both internally as well as with the facts to which the rules are applied. Such 'immanent criticism' is the main instrument of the evolution of thought, and an understanding of this process the characteristic aim of an evolutionary (or critical) as distinguished from the constructivist (or naive) rationalism."[49] This process of immanent criticism is an essential element in the maintenance of the integrity of the legal system. Hayek continues:

> The judge, in other words, serves, or tries to maintain and improve, a going order which nobody has designed, an order that has formed itself without the knowledge and often against the will of authority, that extends beyond the range of deliberate organization on the part of anybody, and that is not based on the individuals doing anybody's will, but on their expectations becoming mutually adjusted. The reason why the judge will be asked to intervene will be that the rules which secure such a matching of expectations are not always observed, or clear enough, or adequate to prevent conflicts even if observed. Since new situations in which the established rules are not adequate will constantly arise, the task of preventing conflict and enhancing the compatibility of actions by appropriately delimiting the range of permitted actions is of necessity a never-ending one, requiring not only the application of already established rules but also the formulation of new rules necessary for the preservation of the order of actions. In their endeavour to cope with new problems by the application of 'principles' which

---

[49]Hayek, *Law, Legislation, and Liberty: Vol. 1*, p. 118.

they have to distil from the *ratio decidendi* of earlier decisions, and so to develop these inchoate rules (which is what 'principles' are) that they will produce the desired effect in new situations, neither the judges nor the parties involved need to know anything about the nature of the resulting overall order, or about any 'interest of society' which they serve, beyond the fact that the rules are meant to assist the individuals in successfully forming expectations in a wide range of circumstances.[50]

The legal system, spurred by new situations requiring new solutions, thus develops out of its internal resources. Continuity – essential to the security of expectations – is maintained, while adaptation is achieved.

Bruno Leoni, in his classic work *Freedom and the Law,* highlighted the importance of the adjudicatory method to legal certainty. He called this the long-run concept of the certainty of law: long-run, because its horizon spanned generations, not merely legislative sessions; because the law could be depended upon to remain constant while undergoing adaptation, rather than be subjected to radical changes at the whim of the legislator. It was a basic characteristic of Roman law.

The Romans accepted and applied a concept of the certainty of the law that could be described as meaning that the law was never to be subjected to sudden and unpredictable changes. Moreover, the law was never to be submitted, as a rule, to the arbitrary will or to the arbitrary power of any legislative assembly or of any one person, including senators or other prominent magistrates of the state. This is the long-run concept, or, if you prefer, the Roman concept, of the certainty of the

---

[50]Hayek, *Law, Legislation, and Liberty: Vol. 1,* pp. 118-119.

law.[51]

The long-run concept also characterized the English common law. The modern concept of legal certainty, on the other hand, is something entirely different. It is the concept of certainty stemming from having the law written down in precise terms. But certainty is more than terminology, for the very statutes expressed in such precise terms can be exchanged for entirely different ones whenever the legislature has a mind to it. Leoni's term for this is the short-run concept of the certainty of the law.

> The certainty of the law, in the sense of a written formula, refers to a state of affairs inevitably conditioned by the possibility that the present law may be replaced at any moment by a subsequent law. The more intense and accelerated is the process of law-making, the more uncertain will it be that present legislation will last for any length of time. Moreover, there is nothing to prevent a law, certain in the above-mentioned sense, from being unpredictably changed by another law no less "certain" than the previous one.
>
> Thus, the certainty of the law, in this sense, could be called the short-run certainty of the law.[52]

The inability to distinguish these two notions has led to much confusion in the debate regarding legal certainty. But the distinction brings into relief the chasm separating these two approaches to law.

James Stoner has written two significant volumes arguing for a recovery of the common law as a standard

---

[51]Leoni, *Freedom and the Law*, pp. 83-84.

[52]Leoni, *Freedom and the Law*, p. 80.

for government.[53] "Common law," he writes, "differs from statute law—and what I call the common law way of thinking differs from legal positivism—not merely in its source or its ground, but more essentially in its perspective. It is law seen from the point of view of a judge faced with a controversy, or a jury seeking to arrive at a verdict, not from the point of view of a sovereign monarch faced with an unmanageable people, or a sovereign people faced with civil war."[54]

This law does not need first to be expressed by a sovereign voice; it is inherent to the situation and the situation's context; it is, Stahl writes, a function of received institutions, principles of justice, and the nature of the case.[55] And it exists as a pre-existing body, to be accepted, not to be created every time afresh. "To judge and jury, law need not begin with a statute, which in turn began with a sovereign authority, which began in consent; popular consent, after all, is given for a reason, and in a democracy it is given by the same sovereign that a jury represents. In court, statutes are law when statutes are there, but new cases come up which statutes do not cover, and, of course, what statutes themselves mean for a case requires interpretation."[56] The law is more than statutes; it is more than that to which, pace Locke and the entire natural-rights tra-

---

[53]James R. Stoner, *Common Law and Liberal Theory: Coke, Hobbes, and the Origins of American Constitutionalism* (Lawrence: University of Kansas Press, 1994); *Common-Law Liberty: Rethinking American Constitutionalism* (Lawrence: University of Kansas Press, 2003).

[54]Stoner, *Common Law and Liberal Theory*, p. 7.

[55]Stahl, *Principles of Law*, pp. 18ff., 22ff., 38ff.

[56]Stoner, *Common Law and Liberal Theory*, p. 7.

dition, the voters have given their immediate consent.[57]

Statute law, in the common-law framework, corrects, amends, and develops the law, within the context of the overall pattern; it must adapt to the law, not vice versa. "From the standpoint of the legislator, case law fills gaps between statutes, for new gaps open as circumstances change; but from the standpoint of the judge, statutes themselves fill gaps and revise precedents, though they are neither as comprehensive nor as precise as their authors might imagine."[58]

Custom, then, conceived as the generation of spon-

---

[57]"Law arises from the consciousness of the people ..., from its valuation of life, its innermost individuality (Savigny), and it arises in consonance with the entire condition of the people, the makeup of the land, climate, extent, means of subsistence, mores (Montesquieu); and precisely because of this, law arises in a living manner in the consciousness of the people, more or less generally known and understandable, or even, where such is not the case, at least generally recognized as that which is peculiar to it and indigenous. All of this taken together can be termed the *popular character of the law*....

By no means does it follow, however, that law must be in agreement with the prevailing opinion and legal point of view of the people. This firstly because the law above all must be in agreement with God's order, with reason and justice, to which even past customs and popular characteristics must be subordinated.... Popular character has its worth as the special peculiar implementation of that which is just and reasonable, not in what it is in itself, and especially not in opposition to the just and the reasonable. Furthermore, popular character is something entirely different from the prevailing opinion of the people; it is the peculiarity implanted in the people and growing during its entire history, the effluence of its divine vocation, and the embodiment of the actual, natural and spiritual requirements of its particular condition. Prevailing opinion, on the other hand, is opinion adopted by the people possibly on the basis of passion and error, which might even be an apostasy from its own popular character...." Stahl, *Principles of Law*, pp. 77-78. See further pp. 83ff.

[58]Stoner, *Common Law and Liberal Theory*, p. 7.

taneous order as overseen by the process of adjudication, and thus an independent source of law, is still the primary force of legal formation in the social order, and will remain so as long as the civil condition exists. The common-law order has custom at its core.

The importance of custom in contemporary society has been highlighted in the work of Hernando de Soto. De Soto points up the crucial significance of custom in economic development, whereby legal institutions have been developed and maintained at the grass-roots level in Third World countries, directly in the teeth of legislation- and codification-bound "formal" legal systems. His book *The Other Path*[59] chronicles the stupendous efforts of poverty-stricken citizens to build economic lives where traditional guarantees of legal security are lacking, because custom-based jural relations are unrecognized. The citizens' solution has been to form their own legal authorities, their own forms of rights and due process, their own legal systems; this has enabled them to maintain a shadow economy, "the informal sector." De Soto estimates the real estate holdings alone of the informal sector world-wide at at least $9.3 trillion.[60] The significance of this "revolution" in the Third World has been leading development experts fundamentally to revise their prescriptions for underdeveloped countries, refocusing their efforts on malfunctioning legal systems. And, last but not least, it appears that indigenous governments may also finally have been getting the message.

Once governments understand that the poor have

---

[59]Hernando de Soto, *The Other Path: The Invisible Revolution in the Third World* (New York: Harper & Row, 1989).

[60]De Soto, *The Mystery of Capital: Why Capitalism Triumphs in the West and Fails Everywhere Else* (New York: Basic Books, 2000), p. 35.

already taken control of vast quantities of real estate and productive economic units, it will become clear that many of the problems they con-
front are the result of the written law not being in
harmony with the way their country actually
works.... The only question that remains is how
soon governments will begin to legitimate these
extralegal holdings by integrating them into an
orderly and coherent legal framework. The alternative is perpetuating a legal anarchy in which the
existing property rights system continually com-
petes with the extralegal one. If these countries
are ever to achieve a single legal system, official
law must adapt to the reality of a massive extralegal push toward widespread property rights.[61]

This is irrefutable evidence that custom as source of law
may be suppressed but cannot be eliminated, regardless of
the pretensions of the omnipotent state.

The role of custom in modern society is further illu-
minated in the work of the economist John R. Commons,
enabled by his emphasis on the interrelationship between
law and economics. Custom, said Commons, is not mere
slavish adherence to received practice; it is the source of
new, more advanced practices, which in turn are received
into the legal system.

One of the ways by which the transition from primitive to modern society is understood is as a supposed shift

---

[61]De Soto, *The Mystery of Capital,* p. 92. A greater mystery even
than the mystery of capital is the mystery of why de Soto in his latter
book, in contrast with *The Other Path,* chose to denigrate Anglo-
American common law and champion none other than codification
as the solution to this legal impasse. But it was codification and
legislation which is what inhibited many Third-World economies,
especially in Latin America, from generating economic growth! De
Soto would have been better off maintaining the neo-mercantilism
motif of *The Other Path.*

from Status to Contract, a notion originally put forward by
Henry Sumner Maine in his classic work *Ancient Law*
(1861). This is misleading, says Commons, if understood
as a transition from "the Age of Custom and Status into
the Age of Contract and Competition." On these terms, it
is said that "in archaic society... people remain in the status, or social class, to which they are born, but in modern
Western civilization they voluntarily fix and terminate their
positions in society by competitive contracts of buying and
selling, hiring and firing, renting, borrowing, etc." In actuality, however, contract does not replace custom, it is another form of custom: "contract, during the past three
hundred years, is also a new custom. He who refuses to
bind himself by contracts, as others do, cannot enter into,
nor continue in, business or employment. Contracts have
become customary and therefore compulsory." The shift
from "status" to "contract" is in fact a shift in the character of indebtedness. "What has happened, economically, is
a change of custom from unreleasable debts to releasable
debts. For, if custom is collective compulsion, it operates
by imposing duties on individuals. Economic duties are
debts, payable in services, or commodities, or purchasing
power. And no individual is free to refuse to become a
debtor if he obtains a living by obtaining control over the
services, commodities, or purchasing power that previ-
ously belonged to others. In modern industrial society nobody obtains a living in any other way. The most powerful
of sanctions, Scarcity, compels him to conform to the customs of the time and place which rate him as a debtor to
those from whom he has acquired whatever, for him, was
scarce." Thus custom had imposed a regime of credit and
debt which the businessman must acknowledge and make
use of, if he is to remain in business. No legislator took it

upon himself to impose these rules.[62]

The courts recognize these changes in business practice and hold them to be customary law. "When a judge or arbitrator looks for a custom as a guide to his decision, what he does is to give an added sanction to the enforcement of the custom.... If the court, in deciding a dispute, looks for its standards to the customs of the neighborhood or of the class of people concerned, or takes 'judicial notice' without formal testimony, or accepts the standards habitually, the court gives to that custom the additional sanction of physical force requiring that the transaction conform to the custom." The court then also integrates the custom into existing law. "But the arbitrator or court goes further in seeking a guide to his decision in a dispute. He looks back to his own previous decisions, or to the decisions of other arbitrators or courts in similar cases, and then endeavors to make his present decision consistent with the preceding decision. This is Precedent. If there is no precedent, or if the precedents are conflicting, or if they are judged to be obsolete, then the arbitrator or court looks again for a custom, or for a principle which he derives from custom, to which, by the process of exclusion and inclusion, he may make his decision conform."[63]

Statute or constitutional law enters the picture, either as a supplement or an alternative to precedent. But even then, this legislation must depend on custom or precedent to be applied to the particular case. "If he does not look to precedent or custom, then his alternative is to look to a statute, by-law, or constitution which, by deliberative action of those in superior authority, had modified the cus-

---

[62]John Rogers Commons, *Institutional Economics: Its Place in Political Economy* (New York: Macmillan, 1934), pp. 703-704.

[63]Commons, *Institutional Economics*, p. 704.

toms or precedents. But even so, these statutory laws are abstract and general, and, before they can be enforced in a particular dispute, they must be construed and interpreted as applicable to the dispute. This interpretation itself therefore goes back to custom or precedent, or habitual assumption, for guidance in applying the statute to the particular case." And therefore custom continues to exercise a powerful influence even in the "age of statutes."[64] This influence can even extend to rendering statute or constitutional law a "dead letter:" "Hence even a statute, constitution, or by-law goes through the scrutiny of custom, precedent, exclusion, and inclusion, in the judicial process of deciding disputes. It may even be that custom or precedent, or habitual assumption, in this process nullifies or modifies statute law and constitutional law. When this occurs completely the law is a 'dead letter.' When it occurs incompletely the law is 'construed.'"[65]

Thus custom embodies a law, not of nature per se, but of human nature: the need for security of expectations.

> Precedent and statute are distinguishing marks of going concerns, but custom and habitual assumptions are the underlying principle of all human relations. Each may even be named a "law," not in the sense of a "law of nature," but in the sense of a law of human nature....They are a law of human nature in that they go to a fundamental and ultimate principle without which man cannot live in society – the principle of Security of Expectations. It is not justice, nor even happiness, that is fundamental – it is security, even the security of injustice and poverty. For insecurity is not so

---

[64]Guido Calabresi, *A Common Law for the Age of Statutes* (Cambridge, MA: Harvard University Press, 1982).

[65]Commons, *Institutional Economics*, p. 704.

much the accidents resulting from the unintentional forces of nature as it is the insecurity of intentions, negligence, and caprice on the part of those having superior physical or bargaining power. The former insecurity can be, and has been, largely avoided by the technological improvements that bring nature's forces under control, but the latter insecurity can be avoided only by stabilization of the wills of those having authority. The extreme case of arbitrary will is slavery. In so far as new customs, precedents, and statutes restrain the wills and assumptions of slave-owners, in so far does liberty encroach on slavery.[66]

This connection between security of expectations and liberty was already in evidence in the medieval common law of land tenure.[67] It is crucial to the maintenance of security, liberty, and equality in the free society.

The doctrine of precedent [in this process]... is a doctrine of logical consistency and equality of treatment. If the arbitrator or court decides a present dispute differently from the decision in similar previous disputes, he is logically inconsistent, and he is treating one person differently

---

[66]Commons, *Institutional Economics,* pp. 704-705.

[67]"This seems the point that is seized by law and that general opinion of which law is the exponent: any considerable uncertainty as to the amount or the kind of the agricultural services makes the tenure unfree. The tenure is unfree, not because the tenant 'holds at the will of the lord,' in the sense of being removable at a moment's notice, but because his services, though in many respects minutely defined by custom, can not be altogether defined without frequent reference to the lord's will." Sir Frederick Pollock and Frederick William Maitland, *The History of English Law Before the Time of Edward I,* 2nd edition, vol. I (Cambridge: At the University Press, 1898), p. 371.

from his treatment of other persons under similar circumstances. This is discrimination, or unequal opportunity. Hence, the doctrine of precedent is the threefold doctrine of security, liberty, and equality — Security, in that it leads to the expectation that disputes will be decided in the future as they have been decided in the past; Liberty, in that subordinate individuals will not be subject to the capricious will of superiors; Equality, in that all individuals of the same class will be treated equally under similar circumstances.[68]

Precedent secures the conditions of security of expectations and equality of treatment, by virtue of its method.

Thus the doctrine of precedent, as a restraint upon the arbitrary will of those in authority, goes to the three most fundamental wishes of mankind: security, liberty, and equality. It is universal for all mankind in all social relations. Even the child appeals to precedent when he complains that his parent treats his other children differently from himself, or treated himself differently yesterday and today. The laborer considers himself victimized when the foreman's friends receive favors which he does not receive. Civil service laws attempt to open up equal opportunity in the public service for all citizens, instead of leaving them to the friends of politicians. The business man appeals to precedent when he charges the railroad company with favoring his competitors by lower rates than those he is required to pay. The legal doctrine that the court is bound by precedent is merely a special case of the universal moral princi-

---

[68]Commons, *Institutional Economics*, p. 705.

ple that everybody should be bound to treat others like himself and like each other under similar circumstances. Otherwise he is capricious, arbitrary, inconsistent.[69]

"Hence, when we speak of the common law we mean, not the technical common law of the legal profession, but the Common Law Method of Making Law by Deciding Disputes." The adjudicatory process is itself formative of law and in fact runs through the warp and woof of the various associations and activities of the civil condition. "The method is not confined to courts of law. It is the method of commercial arbitration and labor arbitration, where the sanctions are not those of sovereignty. It is the method of making law in the family, the church, the labor union, the business concern. It is the method of precedent, choice of customs, unwritten law, and assumptions." The action of binding adjudication maintains the connection between life and law. "Custom becomes common law by the common-law method of deciding disputes, thereby sanctioning what are deemed habitually to be good customs in the act of condemning or not enforcing what are deemed to be bad customs or obsolete customs. Hence, common law is the unwritten law of custom – unwritten because it is found in precedents and habitual assumptions."[70]

This common-law methodology is what separates the United States from the countries of Europe, where legal codes are supreme and court decisions are not formative of the law, and even Great Britain, where the legislature is the supreme authority. In the United States, the courts, particular the supreme courts of the various states

---

[69]Commons, *Institutional Economics,* pp. 705-706.

[70]Commons, *Institutional Economics,* p. 706.

and the federal level, decide which customs will be enforceable as laws, and in fact which statutes will be enforced, and how.

> Since there is no appeal from the Supreme Court, except by the extreme process of constitutional amendment, which requires a three-fourths vote of the states, or by civil war such as that of 1861 which freed the slaves in defiance of the Dred Scott decision, it follows that the court is continually making and remaking the law by the judicial process of deciding disputes. This, for Anglo-Americans, is the common-law method of making law. But in America it reaches a height of authority unknown elsewhere because the Supreme Court is the final authority, superior to legislatures, states, and executives wherever a difference is asserted by the Court itself between its meanings given to words and the meanings given elsewhere.[71]

In the history of the United States, an independent judiciary giving shape to the law in common-law fashion did, in fact, often, though not always, operate in an effective manner as a break on state power, and so to some degree realize the Hayekian ideal of a legal system independent of government. Both Corwin[72] and Dietze[73] have made this argument. But their expositions highlight the

---

[71]Commons, *Institutional Economics,* p. 715.

[72]Chief among many publications: Edward S. Corwin, *The "Higher Law" Background of American Constitutional Law.* Ithaca: Cornell University Press, 1955.

[73]Again, among many: Gottfried Dietze, *America's Political Dilemma: From Limited to Unlimited Democracy* (Baltimore: Johns Hopkins University Press, 1968); *In Defense of Property* (Baltimore: Johns Hopkins University Press, 1963).

instability brought on by an underlying philosophy unable to choose between natural rights and common law proper.[74] This is, of course, precisely the ambiguity that needs to be dispelled.

Commons warned of the need for a proper underlying philosophy to guide an independent judiciary; the thing stands or falls on the interpretations judges give to the keywords of the law.

> It will be seen from the foregoing how urgent it is in the United States, more than it is in other countries, to develop fundamental theories of the correlation of economics, jurisprudence, and ethics. The state and federal supreme courts are final authorities on acts of legislatures in all regulations of property, liberty, and persons under the "due process" clause of the Constitution. The issue usually arises in a suit brought by a citizen or concern against the state or federal officials or legislatures before the Supreme Court, asking for a writ prohibiting the enforcement of the law, on the ground that it conflicts with the Federal Constitution and its Bill of Rights. The Supreme Court, then, on the basis of the findings of fact and the conclusions of the lower court, whether a state supreme court or a lower federal court, passes upon the legislative act or the administrative order, as to whether it conflicts with the superior law of the Constitution. Everything turns on the court's assumption of meanings to be given to property, liberty, person, and due process.[75]

---

[74]Regarding Corwin, one need look no further than Gary L. McDowell, "Coke, Corwin and the Constitution: The 'Higher Law Background' Reconsidered," in *The Review of Politics*, Vol. 55, No. 3, Special Issue on Public Law (Summer, 1993), pp. 393-420.

[75]Commons, *Institutional Economics*, p. 715.

A change in judicial philosophy has totally under-mined the institution of judicial review. Dietze has effectively outlined it. Because the United States originally had come out from under parliamentary despotism, the Founders were more attuned to the possibilities of legisla-tive tyranny, which is why they allowed for the institution of judicial review, willingly submitting to a regime in which legislation could be subordinated, in Dietze's words, to "older constitutional and higher law." This enabled legal protections of the individual. "Thus the judges could pro-tect individual rights from the will of the popular majority. Democratic government was limited and prevented from becoming oppressive." But America proved not to be im-mune to the philosophy of absolute democracy. "With the march of egalitarian democracy, the situation changed. Ju-dicial review as a limitation upon majoritarianism disap-peared more and more, and the way was opened for the advance of a democratic despotism."[76]

The new judicial philosophy which accorded with "democratic despotism" was the so-called sociological ju-risprudence, and its high priest was Oliver Wendell Holmes. The triumph of his viewpoints sounded the death-knell of judicial review as a restraint on runaway government.

> Holmes, stated as early as 1881 that the law "should correspond with the actual feelings and demands of the community, whether right or wrong." Three years later, he said: "Every one instinctively recognizes that in these days the justification of a law for us cannot be found in the

---

[76]Gottfried Dietze, "America and Europe. Decline and Emergence of Judicial Review," in *Virginia Law Review*, Vol. 44, No. 8 (Dec., 1958), pp. 1268-1269.

fact that our fathers always have followed it. It must be found in some help which the law brings toward reaching a social end which the governing power of the community has made up its mind it wants." The necessity of a law which reflected the mutability of social conditions was thus linked up with a rejection of older law.[77]

The American tradition of judicial review has much to recommend it, but its abeyance, indeed, its having been hijacked in service of the all-powerful state, is the result of insufficient attention to the content of the law it purports to uphold.

To this we now turn.

---

[77]Dietze, "America and Europe. Decline and Emergence of Judicial Review," p. 1263.

5. The Common-Law Content

In the beginning was a failure to communicate.

"World history starts from the condition of the most extreme division and animosity among the peoples, the consequence of the confusion of human consciousness."[78] The human condition in its most regressive state is, if not "solitary, poor, nasty, brutish, and short" as Thomas Hobbes put it in *Leviathan,* at least one of group isolation, separatism, autarchy, and monolithic inclusiveness. It is characterized by a friend-foe, "us versus them" mentality. Those within the group have all things in common; "the foreigner," on the other hand, "is still *hostis, exlex.* He is excluded from peaceful intercourse, from juridical and moral relations, as well as from relations of faith."[79] It is the lack of communication, not simply in terms of language but in terms of things, services, and rights,[80] which characterizes life between groups.

---

[78]Stahl, *Die Staatslehre,* §. 2.

[79]Herman Dooyeweerd, *A New Critique of Theoretical Thought: Volume II* (Amsterdam: H.J. Paris, 1955), p. 183.

[80]Compare Althusius' understanding of communication: "This mutual communication, or common enterprise, involves (1) things, (2) services, and (3) common rights *(jura)* by which the numerous and various needs of each and every symbiote are supplied, the self-sufficiency and mutuality of life and human society are achieved, and social life is established and conserved." Johannes Althusius, *Politica. An Abridged Translation of Politics Methodically Set Forth and Illustrated with Sacred and Profane Examples,* ed. and Trans. Frederick S. Carney. Foreword by Daniel J. Elazar (Indianapolis: Liberty Fund, 1995), §. 7.

Common law is what establishes the lines of communication between these erstwhile antagonistic groupings.

It begins with the pursuit of a course of peace
rather than war in the settlement of basic antagonisms.[81]
"The arbitration agreement which developed out of the
agreement for composition between kinship groups, i.e.,
the voluntary submission to a verdict or an ordeal, is not
only the source of all procedural law but also the point of
departure to which even the oldest contracts of private law
can, very broadly speaking, be traced."[82] The original transaction is the settlement of a dispute which otherwise
would be settled by a resort to arms. At this point, there is
no distinction between a felony or a tort, nor between a
tort and a voluntary contract.[83] In fact, "the development
of a unified law of obligations [i.e., contract and tort law]
was certainly derived from the action of tort."[84] These in-

---

[81]"Thus in its beginnings law (in the lawyer's sense) has for
its end, and its sole end, to keep the peace. Other tasks of social
control are left to other agencies – religion and kin discipline or the
public opinion of one's kinsmen or of his brethren in some primitive
brotherhood. The only interest secured by law is the social interest
in the general security in its lowest terms, namely, the interest in
peace and public order. Along with religion and morality it is a
regulative agency by which men are restrained from violent distur-
bance of the general security. It retains this character of a regulative
agency and of a means of which the end is peaceable ordering,
although other ends become manifest as it develops. This end is
sought to be attained by a primitive legal order in three ways: By
regulating self redress and private war, by satisfying, or endeavoring
to satisfy, the desire of the injured party for vengeance, and by
affording some purely mechanical mode of trial which will obviate
all dispute as to the facts." Roscoe Pound, *Jurisprudence*, vol. 1 (St.
Paul, MN: West Publishing Co., 1959), pp. 371-372.
[82]Max Weber, *Economy and Society: An Outline of Interpretive
Sociology*, (Berkeley: University of California Press, 1978), p. 671.
[83]Weber, *Economy and Society*, pp. 647ff.
[84]Weber, *Economy and Society*, p. 678.

voluntary transactions were the first form of transaction, and thus the first form that communication took between groups.

Communication thus takes the form of the establishment of relations. These relations are *jural* relations, or legal transactions. And these transactions are at first involuntary, at least regarding one of the parties; they establish fault, and are resolved through remedying fault. A wrong has been done, creating a relationship of guilt, which must be expiated.

From this form of relationship arises the relationship of debt proper. "The concept of obligation through contract was entirely alien to primitive law; it knew but one form of obligation and claim, viz., that arising *ex delicto* [i.e., from tort].... The *wergilt* debt as set by the judge was the most ancient true debt and all other forms of obligation have derived from it."[85] The voluntary establishment of a debt relationship originally derived from this involuntary debt relationship, and used its forms; at law, a debt was viewed as a wrong which had to be righted. "In England, as late as the Middle Ages, a contractual action was formally connected with a fictitious tort."[86] Only then did the other forms of contract, including sale and purchase, develop.

Already here, with debt obligations as opposed to torts and crimes, the monolithic structure of the group is beginning to give way to a pluriform structure, wherein various groups, chiefly households, stand under a common ruling authority. This transformation has two dimensions: 1) the establishment of a ruling authority – the developing common law requires a ruling authority to implement and

---

[85]Weber, *Economy and Society*, p. 675.
[86]Weber, *Economy and Society*, p. 649; cf. pp. 677-678.

develop it; and 2) the focus on guilt and debt – the original form of jural relation was one in which guilt or debt was incurred, and needed to be absolved.

These jural relations then call up the institution of property. Property, as distinguished from bare possession, envisions the group's holdings as valued by other entities *outside* the group. Within the group, property has no significance, for everything within is held in common or in trust and is subject to the regime of distribution. But holdings take on a new significance within the regime of external communication. And they do so first and foremost as surety or pledge for the debt relations which are the initial forms of jural relations. To be sure, those debt relations were already in existence prior to the development of property, but the surety they required were fulfilled by one's person.[87] Property filled this gap. The significance of property as opposed to bare possession (a distinction which, although fundamental to private law, is universally overlooked) will be highlighted in the discussion of economics. It is simply the capacity to be encumbered, to be used as collateral, above and beyond the utility, physical or otherwise, it might provide.

The result of this development, by which a law is formed establishing a range of "private," actually inter-group, jural relations, by which monolithic groups are displaced by a pluralistic associationalism, is what is called civil society, or, in Oakeshott's terminology, the civil condition.[88] Oakeshott's rhapsody on this condition, wherein human beings are citizens – free and equal parties, rather

---

[87]"Originally the liability for contracted debt, like liability for vengeance and composition, from which it derived, was not a personal liability with one's assets but a liability of the debtor's physical body and of it alone." Weber, *Economy and Society*, p. 680.

[88]Michael Oakeshott, "The Civil Condition," in *On Human Conduct* (Oxford: Oxford University Press, 1975).

than subordinate subjects – wherein the disparate activities of these citizens are coordinated and integrated within the framework of an association of law, is perhaps the most eloquent ever penned. This civil condition provides the frame within which the citizens can pursue particular goals.

Oakeshott distinguishes such universal association from "enterprise associations," formed by citizens for the pursuit of such goals. What distinguishes the civil condition is that it is an association in which individuals as citizens submit to the authority of laws, rather than the pursuit of specific goals.

> Since the civil condition is not enterprise association and since *cives* [i.e., citizens] as such are neither enterprisers nor joint-enterprisers, it follows that they are related solely in terms of their common recognition of the rules which constitute a practice of civility. And the most important postulates of *civitas* stem from this consideration.... They are not the rules of a game the jurisdiction of which is settled in terms of an engagement (like a cricket match) which itself constitutes a relationship. Nor are they the rules of enterprise association which specify conditions alleged to be instrumental to the pursuit of what is already recognized as a common purpose. Here, there is no game being played and there is no common enterprise: association begins and ends in the recognition of rules. Such rules I shall call 'law'... [they are] rules which prescribe the common responsibilities (and the counterpart 'rights' to have these responsibilities fulfilled) of agents and in terms of which they put by their characters as enterprisers and put by all that differentiates them from one another and recognize themselves as formal

equals – *cives.*[89]

This law, which binds the citizens while they pursue their particular goals, and binds the various associations which the citizens may form in the furtherance of those goals, this law to which citizens pledge their allegiance,[90] is common law.

It was already noted above that common law is common precisely because it is what enables a common condition to be shaped between otherwise antagonistic groupings. It is what enables communication and thus a common life; it is what produces the civil condition.

It is, in fact, the law of the *civitas,* the city: the civil condition, *civilitas,* derives from *civitas.*

Gierke has written eloquently of this law of the city

---

[89]Oakeshott, *On Human Conduct,* p. 128.

[90]"The attribution of authority to *respublica* [i.e., the polity embracing the civil condition] and the postulate of the evidential procedure in which the validity of its items may be determined, are nothing other than the acknowledgement of *respublica* as a system of moral (not instrumental) rules, specifying its own jurisdiction, and recognized solely as rules; that is, as conditions to be subscribed to in conduct and binding to consideration independently of their origin or likely or actual outcome in use and of approval of what they prescribe. This authority cannot be acquired in a once-and-for-all endowment but only in the continuous acknowledgement of *cives* who are familiar with the distinction between recognizing a rule and subscribing to its conditions, discerning its utility, or giving approval to what it prescribes. And should it be asked how a manifold of rules, many of unknown origin, subject to deliberate innovation, continuously amplified in judical [*sic*] conclusions about their meanings in contingent situations, not infrequently neglected without penalty, often inconvenient, neither demanding nor capable of evoking the approval of all whom they concern, and never more than a very imperfect reflection of what are currently believed to be 'just' conditions of conduct may be acknowledged to be authoritative, the answer is that authority is the only conceivable attribute it could be indisputably acknowledged to have." Oakeshott, *On Human Conduct,* pp. 153-154.

as it developed in the medieval West: "Free traffic developed and released individual discretion from the fetters with which the particularity of all law to that point had been afflicted. Freedom and flexibility appeared in place of constraint and permanence. In every point a remodeling took place which in general first led to an independent and pure private law, which hitherto had been as unknown as a pure public law.... Among the citizenry, rank ceased to insist on a separate law, and thus instead of the separate laws of estates there emerged a common civil law, just as still today the 'civil' law is likewise the common law."[91] The law of the city became the common law.

The city has always been seen as the source and framework of Western liberty.[92] The standard histories of liberty always began with the Greek city-states, especially Athens, and then moved on to Rome, the city which, we are given to understand, gave law and liberty to the world. Aristotle's description of the civil condition in the *Politics*[93] is still in many ways definitive. But the major source of the civil condition was Rome, the law of which served as the model for the civil condition as it developed in Western Europe.

One crucially important aspect of Rome and its law is that Roman law can be followed in its development from its primitive beginnings to its advanced state.[94] In this

---

[91] Otto Gierke, *Das deutsche Genossenschaftsrecht* [The German Law of Association], vol. 2, p. 646.

[92] For further background on this point, see my book *A Common Law: The Law of Nations and Western Civilization* (Aalten: Pietas Press, 1999), chs. 3 and 5.

[93] See, e.g., Oakeshott's helpful summary: *On Human Conduct*, pp. 110ff.

[94] "Much of the inquiry attempted could not have been prosecuted with the slightest hope of a useful result if there had not existed a body of law, like that of the Romans, bearing in its earliest

sense, at least, it is paradigmatic: for it shows how a common law actually developed from rudimentary beginnings to world-embracing universality.

Dooyeweerd has provided a succinct summary of this development. "The Roman republic started with an elevation of the primitive ancient inter-gentilitial [i.e., inter-clan] law of the Quiritian tribes to a civil law bound to Roman citizenship." In this, Rome did not get very far when it was restricted to its mere internal development; it was only when its rule began embracing the other areas of Italy that it broke out of the shackles of primitive law, to develop a truly common law. "It was only under the influence of the *ius gentium* [i.e., the law applied by Rome to relations among foreign peoples and between them and Roman citizens] that the idea of a *common private law* developed."

> Initially this *ius gentium* did not exceed the boundaries of a law containing the common ingredients in the legal customs of the old Italian tribes. But gradually it emancipated itself from the primitive tribal inter-gentilitial law. In keeping with the expansion of the Roman city-State into a world-empire, the *ius gentium* assumed the characteristic of an integrating world-law founded on the principle of the legal equality of all free men, as legal subjects in the inter-individual legal rela-

---

portions the traces of the most remote antiquity and supplying from its later rules the staple of the civil institutions by which modern society is even now controlled. The necessity of taking the Roman law as a typical system has compelled the author to draw from it what may appear a disproportionate number of his illustrations; but it has not been his intention to write a treatise on Roman jurisprudence, and he has as much as possible avoided all discussions which might give that appearance to his work." Henry Sumner Maine, *Ancient Law* (London: Murray, 1861), preface.

tionships.[95]

In fact, one might say that this law, in addition to Rome's unmatched arms, are what enabled it to establish its empire and maintain it. Which is why the emperor Justinian began his lawbooks with this encomium: "It is expedient that the Imperial Majesty not only be distinguished by arms, but also be protected by laws, so that government may be justly administered in time of both war and peace, and the Roman Sovereign not only may emerge victorious from battle with the enemy, but also by legitimate measures may defeat the evil designs of wicked men and appear as strict in the administration of justice as triumphant over conquered foes."[96]

This common law gave expression to the principles of external, trans-group life, wherein individuals are free, equal, and independent. "The common private law was only led by natural law principles of justice, the 'nature of the matter', legal security, and equity, in their application to the inter-individual legal relationships of men as such." The Roman jurists developed these principles through the process of adjudicating cases arising within the confines of a burgeoning empire. "The *ius gentium* was a typical system of legal rules destined for the decision of lawsuits by the common courts of the State.... In its typical character as an integrating private common law it could not develop outside of the frame-work of the *res publica*, which was only able to *realize* the typical principles of the *ius gentium*."[97] Thus the state as expression of the civil condition, as *res*

---

[95]Dooyeweerd, *New Critique,* vol. III, p. 447.

[96]Justinian, *The Institutes,* in *The Civil Law,* vol. 2, translated and edited by S.P. Scott (Cincinnati: The Central Trust Company, 1932), preamble.

[97]Dooyeweerd, *New Critique,* vol. III, p. 448.

publica, realized – brought to manifestation – these principles in the common law. And it did so, not out of concern
to achieve a purpose of its own, but out of respect for the
inner nature of the law itself; but this, in turn, helped it to
maintain its character as the state.

> This realization was doubtless a matter of public
> interest, although the Roman lawyers emphatically
> established that, as to its inner nature, the com-
> mon private law did not pertain to the *res publica*
> but to the interest of the individual legal subjects
> in their inter-individual relationships. The public
> interest was concerned with the private common
> law insofar as the *res publica,* by means of an im-
> partial common jurisdiction, could prevent a com-
> plete desintegration of private law and a revival of
> the ancient undifferentiated legal spheres; for the
> latter were incompatible with the State's monopo-
> listic organization of the sword-power and the
> public legal authority.[98]

This highlights the importance of the correlation
between the ruling authority standing over the groupings
of society, on the one hand, and the common law integrating those groupings into a society, on the other. The state
in this sense is the correlate of private law, and the two
require each other.

> In this respect the sharp distinction between pub-
> lic and private law was a vital concern of the *res
> publica.* By controlling the jurisdiction over all pri-
> vate law-suits, in as much as they pertained to the
> sphere of common private law, the State was able
> to prohibit any attempt on the part of private
> power-formations to usurp an exclusive authority

---

[98]Dooyeweerd, *New Critique,* vol. III, pp. 448-449.

over the subjects of the body politic. Since the common private law was also sharply distinguished from all internal private legal spheres of a typical non-juridical qualification, its formation was by the nature of the case *bound* to the *res publica*.[99]

Apart from the state as *res publica*, as polity embodying the civil condition, then, the common law cannot develop. As far as the private spheres were concerned internally, "there was not any room for an inter-individual common legal sphere based upon the natural law principle of equality of all free individuals as such. As to their inner nature the non-political societal relationships nowhere corresponded to this principle. But with respect to the State this principle was the natural correlate of the principle of the public legal equality of its subjects as to their common subjection to the public authority."[100] These distinctions are crucial to understanding the nature of private law as the means by which private groups are kept private, kept from themselves becoming overweening powers, but rather mutually integrated and coordinated.

It is this law, as embodied in the *Corpus Iuris Civilis*, which Rome gave to the world, and which was received with gusto in the medieval West. It formed the basis for a new *Ius Commune*, or common law, which is a fascinating story in itself: fascinating not only because of the audacity of the attempt, or at least the ideal, to make use of the law of the Roman cosmopolis within the framework of feudal kingdoms, but also for the lessons that the attempt teaches regarding the imperviousness of Europe to such a law, the intransigence of monarchies and princedoms, aristocracies

---

[99]Dooyeweerd, *New Critique*, vol. III, p. 449.
[100]Dooyeweerd, *New Critique*, vol. III, p. 449.

and nobilities, to a law establishing freedom and equality at its heart.[101]

The common law did make headway in Europe; and it did so in a rather subversive manner, working within the framework of privilege and the constitution of estates of which the polities of Europe were formed;[102] this being a major subject of discussion in a forthcoming book of mine,[103] I will not enter further into it, but rather focus on the polity which in many ways mirrored Rome, and which, uniquely in Europe, developed its own common law, and its own civil condition.[104]

England has always been viewed as a precocious exception to the general development of law and state in Europe, but that is to misconstrue its uniqueness. It was not an exception, but the leader in the kinds of developments the other nations of Europe pursued only haltingly.

---

[101]An excellent overview of this phenomenon is contained in Manlio Bellomo, *The Common Legal Past of Europe, 1000-1800*, trans. Lydia G. Cochrane (Washington, DC: The Catholic University of America Press, 1995).

[102]For a fascinating overview of the history of the conflict of principles and frameworks in Western Europe, see Oakeshott, *On Human Conduct*, ch. III, "On the Character of a Modern European State."

[103]*Covenant & Capital*, forthcoming.

[104]The usual way of comparing English common law with Roman law is to advert to the English lawyer's success in warding off the influence of Roman law, as opposed to his counterpart on the continent, where the native laws in fact succumbed in one degree or another to the (oft times depicted as nefarious) influence of Roman law. In fact, the situation should be viewed entirely differently: English common law developed in England as a cognate legal system to Roman law, performing the same functions as Roman law, the conditions there, as we shall see, being propitious for this; while on the Continent, the conditions not being propitious, native law struggled to develop in the direction of a common law, and Roman law was resorted to as a sort of cudgel to move the various fragmentary, particularistic legal systems in that direction.

The legal order of Europe in the Middle Ages was, in the main, feudal, which means that it combined landholding with political power. To be put in possession of a set piece of territory was to be entrusted with a set range of political responsibilities. The two went together. Furthermore, there was a hierarchy established, from the supreme lord, usually the king, at the apex, to the serf on the ground, establishing a relationship of lord-vassal (and, at the bottom, lord-serf). At the apex, the king held all the land. He distributed the land among a group of chief vassals, in exchange for the performance of duties towards him. These vassals, in turn, ruled their lands, they were lords; and they distributed their lands among their own set of vassals, in exchange for performance of duties. And so it went, all the way down to the level of the manor, the basic unit of the feudal economy, wherein the lord distributed the land among a group of serfs who were bound to the land and obligated to perform services to him. The entire structure was covenantal, embodying reciprocal rights and duties; even the serfs were not without rights vis-a-vis their lords.[105]

What distinguished the English development from that on the continent is that the English king never allowed this feudal hierarchy to stand in the way of a direct relationship between him and his subjects. There always remained this direct connection. Maitland summarizes the key distinctions:

> [William] exacted an oath of fealty not merely from his own tenants, but from all the possessors of land, no matter whose men they were; they were to be faithful to him against all other men,

---

[105]On reciprocal rights and duties, see Berman, *Law and Revolution*, pp. 304ff., 322ff.

even against their lords. This became fundamental
law ... whenever homage or fealty was done to
any mesne lord, the tenant expressly saved the
faith that he owed to his lord the king. The oath
of allegiance we find is exacted from all men; this
exaction becomes part of the regular business of
the local courts....[106]

Hence, the political bond, the oath of allegiance, is
taken from all landholders, regardless of feudal allegiance.
This contrasted with the situation in France, for example,
where the king only obtained an oath of allegiance from
his immediate vassals; the latter's vassals only swore an
oath of allegiance to their immediate lords.[107]

Here, from Maitland, are other examples of direct
relation between king and subject:

Taxation is not feudalized. The king for a while is
strong enough to tax the nation, to tax the
sub-tenants, to get straight at the mass of the peo-

---

[106]F.W. Maitland, *The Constitutional History of England* (Cambridge: Cambridge University Press, 1908), p. 161.

[107]"The sole connection between the king and these
sub-vassals would be a mediate connection, only through their lord
would he control them. C who held of B who held of A who held
of the king would not be the king's man or have any place in a court
or assembly over which the king presided; he would not even be A's
man; he would never meet or sit along with A's tenants on a footing
of legal equality ; he would owe no fealty or homage to any one but
his immediate lord, namely, B. This ideal of a perfectly feudalized
society was pretty fully realized in France; no immediate bond bound
the vassals of the Duke of Normandy to the king of the French; they
were bound to the Duke, and the Duke to the king. Happily this
ideal is but very imperfectly realized in England, this we must
constantly notice; but we ought carefully to keep this ideal in mind,
for there have been powerful forces making for its realization and
they have had to be met not only by laws, but also by the sword."
Maitland, *Constitutional History*, pp. 38-39.

ple, their lands and their goods, without the intervention of their lords.... The king deals with the
smaller landowners in the county court, until at
last the county court is represented at Westmin-
ster by knights of the shire. On the other hand,
the king relying on the nation is strong enough to
insist that the lords shall not tax their tenants
without his consent.... The old local courts are
kept alive, and are not feudal assemblies. The jurisdiction of the feudal courts is strictly limited;
criminal jurisdiction they have none save by express royal grant, and the kings are on the whole
chary of making such grants. Seldom, indeed, can
any lord exercise more than what on the continent would have been considered justice of a very
low degree.... Before the middle of the thirteenth
century [the king's] courts have practically become courts of first instance for the whole realm
– from Henry II's day his itinerant justices have
been carrying a common law through the land....
When the time for a representative parliament has
come, the smaller tenants in chief are mixed with
their own sub-vassals, and the bodies which are
represented by the knights of the shire are the
county courts in which all freeholders find a
place. The model parliament of 1295 follows
closely on the great statute of 1290 (*Quia
Emptores*), which puts a stop to subinfeudation,
and vastly diminishes the public importance of
tenure.[108]

Through this emphasis on direct relation, especially
as mediated through the adjudicatory process and the royal
courts, the English kings established a common-law regime which broke down monolithic social structures re-

---

[108]Maitland, *Constitutional History*, pp. 162-163.

stricting individuality, replacing them with relations answering to the civil condition. Alan Macfarlane's groundbreaking work, *The Origins of English Individualism*, details this transformation in the sphere of land tenure.[109] The English became a nation of individualists from very early on, corresponding to a regime of common-law rights and duties in which hierarchy was replaced by equality. The estate, which on the continent embodied the idea of rank,[110] in England came to relate to the landholding. "The peculiarly English character of this metamorphosis of feudal landholding from politics to property is testified to by the fact that, in English, the word estate came to mean landed or other property, while, in French, its cognate continued up to the time of the Revolution to indicate the major class, or rank, to which a person belonged. In England tenure overruled status, while on the Continent status overruled tenure."[111]

This basic equality of status gave rise to a system of representation unique in Europe, answering to the civil condition. As these freeholders were taxed by the king, they gained a forum of representation, the House of Commons, whereby these taxes could be approved in exchange

---

[109]Alan Macfarlane, *The Origins of English Individualism: The Family, Property, and Social Transition* (Oxford: Basil Blackwell, 1978).

[110]As in "the estates of the realm." The estates on the continent were occupational groups with status attaching to occupation. The first estate was the clergy; the second was the nobility; the third was the so-called *bourgeoisie*. These estates were represented politically in separate chambers. This was part of the "balkanization" of the social order – the other form of balkanization being provincialism, a spinoff of feudal mediate relations, whereby the king only indirectly related to his dominions.

[111]C. Reinold Noyes, *The Institution of Property: A Study of the Development, Substance and Arrangement of the System of Property in Modern Anglo-American Law* (New York: Longman, Green, & Co., 1936), p. 248.

for input in government. The link of taxation with representation was forged on a citizen basis.

As this framework answered to the civil condition, it more and more took on the trappings of a *civitas*, of a republic proper. The English monarch became ever more the servant of the House of Commons, until the polity became a republic in everything but name. And the foundation of this polity was the unified common law establishing a fundamental equality and liberty of citizens, enshrined in a series of recognized rights, the body of which grew up through the adjudicatory process. In this manner, the common-law regime was a part of the constitution of the polity; the constitution was never a body of public law considered in isolation from this essentially private-legal order, but an integrated whole, whereby the institutions of public law were coordinate with and interwoven with the institutions of private law.

Now, as we have seen, the advent of natural-rights political philosophy upset this state of affairs. It introduced the notion of a constitution as an explicit contract or agreement between citizens and the state, whereby the state was called into existence by the erstwhile state-less citizens, on the basis of a social contract. The contract is the constitution; and, in line with the natural-rights philosophy, it erects its own form of a barrier to overweening government, in the form of the separation of powers. Yet in its rationalistic shortsightedness, by which it looked askance at that which was historical, the product of a myriad of incremental steps rather than a preconceived plan, it severed the link to the common-law order upon which historical constitutionalism and the web of rights and liberties was based.

The body of rights and liberties which Americans enjoyed originally had come with them from England, and it did so as an inheritance. English liberty was a *birthright*.

As Christopher Brooke, a leading member of the House of Commons in the early 17th century, put it: "We hold our privileges by prescription and prescription is inheritance."[112]

William Penn (1644-1718) placed great stock in this inherited constitution. The rights of Englishmen were a great good: "Above all Kingdoms under Heaven, it is *England's* Felicity to have her Constitution so impartially Just and Free, as there cannot well be any Thing more remote from Arbitrariness, and Zealous of preserving the Laws, by which it's Rights are maintained."[113] Basic to this constitution are fundamental laws, of which the first part is the general principles held in common among all nations.-[114] The second, however, pertains to Englishmen in particular:

> But those Rights and Priviledges, which I call *English,* and which are the proper *Birth-Right* of *Englishmen,* and may be reduced to these Three.
> I. *An Ownership, and Undisturbed Possession: That what they have, is Rightly theirs, and no Body's else.*
> II. *A Voting of every Law that is made, whereby that Ownership or Propriety may be maintained.*
> III. *An Influence upon, and a Real Share in that Judica-*

---

[112]Corinne C. Weston, "England: Ancient Constitution and Common Law," in *The Cambridge History of Political Thought: 1450-1700,* p. 377.

[113]"England's Present Interest Considered," in *The Political Writings of William Penn,* p. 26.

[114]"the Corner-Stones of Humane Structure, the Basis of Reasonable Societies, without which all would run into Heaps and Confusion; to wit, Honestè [*sic*] vivere, Alterum non laedere, jus suum cuique tribuere, that is, To live honestly, not to hurt another, and to give every one their Right, (Excellent Principles, and common to all Nations)." "England's Present Interest Considered," in *The Political Writings of William Penn,* p. 26.

*tory Power that must apply every such Law, which is the
Ancient Necessary and Laudable Use of Juries: If not
found among the* Britains, *to be sure Practised by the*
Saxons, *and continued through the* Normans *to this very
Day.*

That these have been the Ancient and Undoubted
Rights of *Englishmen*, as Three great Roots, under
whose Spacious Branches the *English People* have
been wont to shelter themselves against the
Storms of Arbitrary Government, I shall
endeavour to prove.[115]

English rights and liberties were precisely those which established the citizen in his liberty and property, and guar-
anteed him due process of law, thus those which enabled
him to function as a citizen. The public-legal order existed
to maintain and support this private-legal order.

This inherited constitution – we repeat – was
brought over by the Englishmen who founded the New
World colonies of Virginia, Massachusetts Bay, and those
which followed. Americans were Englishmen, endowed
with the rights thereto accruing, and the English common
law was the law of the land on both sides of the Atlantic.
This understanding was reflected in the first of the American revolutionary documents, the *Resolutions of the Stamp
Act Congress* of 1765, which declared "That his majesty's
subjects in these colonies, owe the same allegiance to the
crown of Great Britain, that is owing from his subjects
born within the realm, and all due subordination to that
august body, the parliament of Great Britain," and, con-
currently, "That his majesty's liege subjects in these colonies are entitled to all the inherent rights and privileges of
his natural born subjects within the kingdom of Great Brit-

---

[115]"England's Present Interest Considered," in *The Political
Writings of William Penn*, pp. 26-27.

ain."

Only 11 years later, however, matters had changed dramatically. For in the Declaration of Independence, "the actions of that monarch were declared to be in violation of the inalienable rights of man; they had as their object the establishment of an absolute tyranny over the states. No mention was made... of the rights of Englishmen."[116] The leaven of natural rights had permeated the American colonies, just as it had permeated all of Western civilization. Historical rights had given way to natural rights. On the continent, legal philosophy was being conducted entirely in this key.

England, too, had undergone that influence, but its common law had not been subjected to the codification efforts of the continent, efforts in which the legal order was viewed as springing whole out of the head of the legislator. The inherent conflict between historic and natural-rights doctrines in England had slumbered beneath the surface. It took the outbreak of the French Revolution and Edmund Burke's celebrated response (published as *Reflections on the Revolution in France)* to burst the bubble of harmony. From this point on, the conflict between historic and natural rights was out in the open for all to see.

In the Declaration of Independence, natural rights likewise provided the legitimation of the *novus ordo seclorum* known as the United States of America, but in an entirely different manner than with the French Revolution. The American revolutionaries were not interested in overthrowing the received order; they were interested, rather, in maintaining their received institutions, customs, and laws in the face of an overweening British monarchy and parliament. But, undeniably, there was more to the American revolutionary movement than prescriptive rights. The

---

[116]Perry, *Sources of Our Liberties,* p. 318

natural-rights-based theory originating in Grotius had here borne significant fruit: "Many of the Revolutionary patriots believed with Thomas Dickinson that liberties do not result from charters; charters rather are in the nature of declarations of pre-existing rights."[117] Yet, although both the American and the French Revolution partook of the elixir of inalienable natural rights, the underlying constitutions which they established were of a fundamentally different sort. Post-revolutionary France had put paid to its feudal past; America, on the other hand, had carried out "a conservative counter-revolution."[118]

And so matters stand, at bottom, to this day. The American Revolution established a common-law regime upon the basis of natural rights. It is a relationship which, given the above understandings, is, to say the least, problematic, but one which has received scant attention.[119] Conservatives of all people need to re-evaluate the extremely precarious situation it has produced.

On the continent, the Revolution led to the essential overthrow of historic institutions and the impoverishment of law through the establishment of Jacobin institutions of representation and bureaucracy and incessant efforts at the codification of the law.

This has led to the situation today, in which two

---

[117]Haines, *The Revival of Natural Law Concepts*, ch. II, sec. 2.

[118]Rushdoony, *This Independent Republic*, p. 21.

[119]One exception is formed by the work of Stoner (cf. p. 39 above). For example: "How can any sort of political liberty consistent with the republican principle of the sovereignty of the people, which the Constitution announces in its first words and which popular elections seem to reinforce, be attached to inherited law that preserves a certain independence from popular will?... In a sense it is the burden of this entire study to give a satisfactory answer to the question of the relation of popular sovereignty to political liberty anchored in common law." *Common Law & Liberal Theory*, p. 8.

traditions stand against each other, each claiming to represent Western civilization, indeed world order: the
common-law tradition, headed by the United States, and
the civil-law tradition, headed by the European Union.
Having detailed this opposition in a previous book,[120] I
refer the reader to that work.

The conflict between these two traditions has taken
place mainly at the level of economics, to which we now
turn.

---

[120] *A Common Law.*

6. Battleground Economy

Having established beyond a reasonable doubt the ineffectiveness of the separation of powers to bridle the power of the state, it is time to examine the consequences of that unbridled power. Proponents of state power view this unfetteredness as a great good. Unfettered state power was already in evidence in the past few years of a Democrat-led Congress. It is entirely on display with the Obama administration.

The clearest example of overreach in this regard is the recent credit crisis, which also demonstrates the counterproductiveness of state power *over* law, as opposed to state power coordinate *with* law.

The usual explanation of this crisis has been the failure of capitalism. The free market led to unbridled greed on the part of traders, bankers, homeowners, mortgage lenders, etc. The pursuit of filthy lucre (apparently something new in history) led to the breakdown of the financial system, with only the government capable of restoring that system's viability. As President Obama put it, "Only government can break the vicious cycles that are crippling our economy – where a lack of spending leads to lost jobs which leads to even less spending; where an inability to lend and borrow stops growth and leads to even less credit."[121]

The solution proposed by the Obama administration, and the Federal Reserve in tow, was to engage in classic Keynesian deficit spending. The problem was a lack of

---

[121]Speech at George Mason University, January 8th, 2009.

demand, brought about by less borrowing, either for investment or for consumption. The response, straight out of 1950s-era macroeconomics textbooks, was to "prime the pump," to use the "power of government" to "jump-start" demand. As Obama put it: "The last thing a government should do in the middle of a recession is to cut back on spending. You see, when this recession began, many families sat around the kitchen table and tried to figure out where they could cut back. So have many businesses. This is a completely reasonable and understandable reaction. But if everybody, if every family in America, if every business in America cuts back all at once, then no one is spending any money which means there are no customers which means there are more layoffs, which means that the economy gets even worse. That's why the government has to step in and temporarily boost spending in order to stimulate demand."[122]

What this means is that government power is needed to avert the otherwise counterproductive workings of the private-law regime. Credit is not being engaged, which points to market failure; the government steps in to fill the gap. At least this Keynesian prescription has the merit of recognizing the importance of credit and debt to economics, something entirely lacking in traditional free-market economic theory. But it does not rightly understand credit and debt; if it did, it would not be so keen to intervene in these functionings. For the ebb and flow of credit is the result of necessary responses to real-world conditions, to evaluations of concrete future prospects, not to the wishes of politicians or to the will of a flattered electorate.

---

[122]Speech on the state of the economy, April 14th, 2009 – a speech which, in its outline of the alleged origins of the credit crisis, is shocking in its disingenuousness.

Credit and debt are the fulcrum of the common law, the major form taken by jural relations. As was discussed earlier, the common law embodies a range of jural relations facilitating communication between erstwhile hostile groupings, leading to the liberation of the individual from the smothering embrace of monolithic group life, into pluralistic associationalism – the civil condition. The core of these jural relations is credit and debt, first involuntary debt – fault – then voluntary credit and debt – loan. This invokes the institution of property, as surety in these bonds of commitment, and finally the range of other contracts, including purchase and sale (see pp. 54-56 above).

Thus, the basic relation of economics is not buying and selling, but borrowing and lending; this forms the basis for all the production and consumption, all the buying and selling, that occurs in the market.[123] What this furthermore means is that the basic economic relation is not the transitory, ephemeral kind established through purchase and sale, but long-term relations established through credit and debt, by which commitments are forged which shape life situations in an ongoing fashion. These commitments are freely engaged, rather than imposed.[124] They form the backbone of the free society and the civil condition, and

---

[123]The work of Heinsohn and Steiger, virtually unknown in the English-speaking world, is of fundamental importance here. They have reworked economic theory in terms of this basic understanding. See Gunnar Heinsohn and Otto Steiger, *Eigentum, Zins und Geld: Ungelöste Rätsel der Wirtschaftswissenschaft* [Property, Interest, and Money: Unsolved Mysteries of Economic Science], 5th edition (Marburg: Metropolis Verlag, 2008). Helpful English-language summaries are provide in *Property Economics*, ed. Otto Steiger (Marburg: Metropolis Verlag, 2008); Gunnar Heinsohn and Otto Steiger, "The Property Theory of Interest and Money," in J. Smithin (ed.), *What is Money?* (London: Routledge, 2000).

[124]Recall Commons' statement regarding the shift from unreleasable to releasable debts, p. 43 above.

enable it to function. Without them, the return to autarchy and monolithic, command-based group life beckons.

If the common law establishes the lines of communication, it is money which functions as the circulating medium, the life-blood of the societal (as opposed to communal)[125] organism. The rights of property and obligation, whether contract or tort, in order to judge their relative significance, have a value attached to them, expressed in money terms. The transactions embodied in jural relations are engagements of valuation, and money is the medium of that valuation. Money is the means of extinguishing obligation; this is why demand for it exists; obligation is extinguished by providing equivalent value.

On the basis of this fact, the German and Dutch common-law, pre-codification traditions developed a unique terminology expressive of this reality, dubbing all such rights *asset-rights* (German: Vermögensrechte; Dutch: vermogensrechten), these rights being reducible to money value. Savigny, the great German common-law philosopher, cogently expressed this significance:

> This purely quantitative treatment of assets, apart from which any maintenance of rights would be possible in only an extremely imperfect manner, is mediated by the concept of *value*, or the equation

---

[125]*Community versus society* is a standard opposition in sociology. It refers back to the classic work of Ferdinand Tönnies, *Gemeinschaft und Gesellschaft* (1887), wherein this opposition is the theme, and in which community as organized, purpose-driven group life is elevated above amoral, purposeless society as embodied in the civil condition. The seeds for this manner of thinking were already sown by G.W.F. Hegel in his *Grundlinien der Philosophie des Rechts,* when he argued that the state as "ethical substance" rectified the shortcomings of egotistical civil society; hereby Hegel showed himself to be oblivious to the reality of the situation, whereby the state and civil society are coeval and mutually reinforcing.

of different asset-rights through reduction to a common denominator. And this concept in turn is externally manifested and introduced in common life by *money,* such that value and money value are equivalent expressions, and in fact are customarily used interchangeably. The individual asset is thus transformed in this manner into a pure quantity, such that all of its components are dissolved in the ownership of sums of money: thus, property in any other thing – all manner of property rights, extending to the mere use of a thing, naturally with special consideration to the duration thereof – finally, obligations as well, thus claims and debts, whether they are directed to the acquisition of property rights and their mere enjoyment or not. This makes it possible to reduce even the pure obligation the object of which is undefined, to true property, so that the individual asset can always be conceived either as ownership of a sum of money, or as an invaluable money debt, or as entirely worthless. At the same time, a more definite meaning can be given to the remark made at the start of this section, that not all acts are equally suited to be objects of obligations: to wit, those acts for which the conversion into money sums are entirely unthinkable are not suitable thereto; at the least, these can only be viewed as obligations only improperly, and in incomplete manner.[126]

Along the same lines, Stahl classified these rights as "property in the broad sense."[127]

---

[126]Friedrich Karl von Savigny, *System des heutigen Römischen Rechts* [System of the Modern Roman Law], vol. 1 (Berlin: Veit, 1840), pp. 376-378.

[127]Stahl, *Private Law,* p. 43.

Money is, one might say, a by-product of the jural relations established through the common law. It is produced as part of the same process by which legal obligations, commitments, exchanges come about, it being an essential element of the process; it is more than a mere extraneous commodity to facilitate exchange; rather, it is essential to the very process of obligation and commitment, it being the means through which obligations are extinguished. It is sometimes thought that money is a special form of debt;[128] that is not the case, but it is unbreakably linked with debt, the two being part of the same process of engagement and extinguishment of obligation.

Money is thus issued as part of the workings of the rights-generating legal order. It is the medium of communicating value, precisely for the purpose of extinguishing obligation. The process of valuation, of obtaining an equality of reference across the myriad activities and groupings in a society, is, at bottom, what the common-law regime is all about. Commons' work makes this clear: for him, the key concept in law and economics is the common-law doctrine of "reasonable value," as developed by the courts.

Valuation is obtained not only through the issue of

---

[128]"Thus, clearly, money and goods are not the same thing but are, on the contrary, exactly opposite things. Most confusion in economic thinking arises from failure to recognize this fact. Goods are wealth which you have, while money is *a claim on wealth* which you do not have. Thus goods are an asset; money is a debt. If goods are wealth; money is not wealth, or negative wealth, or even anti-wealth. They always behave in opposite ways, just as they usually move in opposite directions. If the value of one goes up, the value of the other goes down, and in the same proportion. The value of goods, expressed in money, is called 'prices,' while the value of money, expressed in goods, is called 'value.'"Carroll Quigley, *Tragedy and Hope: A History of the World in Our Time* (New York: Macmillan, 1966), p. 44.

money but also through the issue of court decisions, which settle the matter by dictating redress; they both have this common root, to wit, the result of appeal to adjudicate on a point of uncertainty, indicating a disparity of valuation. This highlights why the adjudicatory process is to be preferred above the decree-oriented imputation of the legislative process. The process of adjudicated valuation establishes the points of reference which then become binding on society at large.

How is money the result of adjudication? Firstly, it springs from a certain specific form of contract, and contracts, to be binding, must be upholdable in court. So then, behind the formation of money is the power of the legal order, apart from which it would not have validity; nor would any other contract.

Furthermore, money is issued in a process of contracting by which its value is established, not by fiat, but by convention and agreement.

At bottom, money is a claim against the issuer's property. The holder of money may redeem it for that property. This is what maintains the value of that money. Further, it is an anonymized claim, which means that although the issuer is named, the recipient is not: money may pass from hand to hand and be used by any holder, unlike, e.g., a check, which can only be cashed by the recipient named on it. Thus it serves as the univeral means for extinguishing obligations.

Why would anyone issue money in the first place? For the money, of course. Because by doing so, the issuer can charge interest for the money he issues.

The recipient of the money – the debtor – promises to repay the sum borrowed, plus interest. Furthermore, in order to receive credit, he encumbers his own property, as collateral for the sum received. In so doing, he gains liquidity while keeping control of the property concerned.

Hence, the economy runs on two levels simultaneously: the level of credit and debt, and the level of production and consumption. "[In credit-debt relations,] goods and resources are neither transferred nor touched. Creditors and debtors continue to acquire the returns of the material yield due to the possessional rights to their resources. Credit operations, thus, never interfere with the physical use of resources, but only deal with titles to property."[129]

Valuation as a market function is inherent to this money-issuing, credit-generating process. Valuation is not first attained through the process of buying and selling, but through the process of encumbering, collateralizing, and issuing money in credit contracts. This is because credit contracts, not sales contracts, are original.

> Property titles are always transferred in creditor-debtor contracts in which both creditor and debtor are proprietors. These contracts are divided into mere *credit contracts* and *sales contracts*. In the former, claims to property are transferred but not claims to possession, rights to the physical use of goods or resources. In the latter, claims to property are transferred *uno actu* with claims to possession. Sales contracts are always subordinated to the credit contracts whose fulfilment they serve.[130]

The issue itself forms the original valuation, for money is issued in terms of the value of the collateral. The property put up as collateral receives its valuation in the credit contract through which money is obtained.

---

[129]Heinsohn, and Steiger, "The Property Theory of Interest and Money," in *What Is Money?*, p. 82.

[130]Heinsohn and Steiger, "The Property Theory of Interest and Money," in *What Is Money?*, p. 82.

Valuation being inherent in the issue of money, it is not dependent on the previous valuation of any commodity but instead is the source of the valuation of commodities. Contemporary goods-based economic theory, viewing money as the "most marketable commodity" (Carl Menger's classic formulation), usually views the precious metals, preeminently gold, as the standard by which to value everything else. But this is to put the cart before the horse; and, viewing things from this angle it is easy to understand some economists' impatience:

> Hundreds of years of "value theory" tradition make it difficult to understand that investigation into the origin of the value of economic goods is not a scientific question. Economic science has difficulty divesting itself of that medieval insistence on investigating the *substance* of things, in order, in the manner of natural science since the Enlightenment, to move on to investigating the *relations* between economic phenomena. For this it requires no classical or neoclassical value mysticism. The value of economic goods is measured in differentiable money units in no other way than temperature is in various degree scales. Establishing a currency unit is an act just like establishing the Celsius scale for the measurement of temperature. Why the temperature difference between two aggregate conditions of water is divisible in one hundred equal intervals cannot be answered scientifically. Not only three but a thousand, yea innumerable foundations were possible for measuring temperature; it is only convention that made use of the decimal system of 100 sections for the scale.[131]

---

[131]Stadermann and Steiger, *Schulökonomik*, p. 15.

The value of things is not inherent in certain things, in order to serve as the basis for the valuation of all other
things. Valuation is a matter of convention and agreement,
of function, not substance: it is an affair of common-law
functionality.

We are a far cry from Keynesian prescriptions of
demand-side government stimulus. The role of the sovereign is not to act to override the mechanisms of valuation
inherent in the legal order when the signals they send are
unpleasant, but rather to uphold them in common-law
fashion. But, as has been noted over and over again by
freedom-loving economists and legal philosophers, the
statist orientation by which state power subjugates the legal order is motivated precisely by the desire to override
and short-circuit this valuation, in order to replace it by
"the will of the people," which, as we have seen, is nothing
other than the will of horse-trading interest groups seeking
to extract particular benefit when they cannot earn it in an
honest manner.

The recent credit crisis forms an egregious example
of such intervention. From the start, the mechanisms of
valuation were abused, eventually to the point where the
system virtually froze up. And the underlying motivation
was none other than another form of natural rights, this
time in the guise of "affordable housing." This
government-led agenda to open "the American Dream" to
low-income families was just another instance of the attempt to undercut the mechanisms of valuation through
state-imposed fiat.[132]

The vehicle for accomplishing this goal was the sub-

---

[132]The Carter-era Community Reinvestment Act and the
Clinton-era National Homeownership Strategy are two centerpieces
of this effort.

prime loan. Such loans, by which mortgage borrowing was opened up to borrowers unable to meet traditional standards of solvency, were illegal before 1980. New legislation allowed for higher rates and fees to be charged on mortgages, offsetting the increased risk of default.[133] Further legislation allowing for mortgage interest-rate deduction made these loans a viable option, leading to a large-scale market for them. The market only began booming, however, when these mortgages began to be packaged into so-called Mortgage-Backed Securities (MBS) through the process known as securitization. Essentially, these subprime loans were mixed together with lower-risk loans in order to spread, and so minimize, the risk of the package as a whole. On top of that, government-sponsored entities (GSEs: Fannie Mae, Freddie Mac) actively traded in the market for mortgages, acting as a go-between in the securitization process and implicitly guaranteeing the risk involved, leading market actors to treat these securities as investment-grade, thus capable of being used as the basis of further lending.[134] In this manner, the asset base upon

---

[133]Souphala Chomsisengphet and Anthony Pennington-Cross, "The Evolution of the Subprime Mortgage Market," in *Federal Reserve Bank of St. Louis Review,* January/February 2006, 88 (1), p. 38.

[134]Here is a succinct account of the matter: "Mortgage-backed securities (MBS) are primarily 'agency' securities issued by a government agency such as Ginnie Mae or a government-sponsored enterprise such as Fannie Mae or Freddie Mac. These agencies typically guarantee the interest and principal payments on their securities and are considered to offer strong credit quality due to their access to lines of credit from the U.S. Treasury. The mortgage-backed securities market also includes 'private-label' mortgage securities issued by subsidiaries of investment banks, financial institutions and home builders, but these represent a small portion of the total mortgage-backed securities outstanding." *About MBS/ABS,* from the Investing in Bonds web site (investinginbonds.com).

which the financial system rests was fatally undermined.

This market never would have boomed without the implicit government guarantee of the trillions of dollars of mortgages essentially laundered by the GSEs. With this guarantee, investment banks marketed these assets with gusto to financial institutions and every manner of investor the world over. Each of these packages contained within its inner recesses the ticking time bomb of subprime mortgage default. Instead of the risk being spread and so minimized through the process of securitization, it spread as an infection throughout the financial system.

The resulting seizure of credit markets, failure of banks and other lending institutions, and general collapse in economic activity, was supposed to be met by addressing the underlying problem – the infiltration of bad assets onto balance sheets across the board – through a program known as the Troubled Assets Relief Program (TARP). But instead of being used to buy up "troubled assets," the money was used to expand the government's ownership of private entities, including banks, insurance companies, and automobile companies. The "troubled assets" which the government had done so much to bring into the world became its excuse for taking over vast swathes of the private sector.

In this way, the natural-rights philosophy which dominates the political mindset (in the form of an implicit right of homeownership) inspired a misguided agenda which first crippled the private sector, and then was used as a pretext by the government to assume control of the private sector.

And while economics forms the battleground upon which the struggle for liberty is waged, the roots of that

---

URL: http://www.investinginbonds.com/
learnmore.asp?catid=11

struggle go far deeper, indeed into the inner recesses of the human heart.

7. The Religious Root of the Social Question

The battle between constitutionalism and absolutism, fought out during the 16th and 17th centuries and apparently ending in the triumph of constitutionalism, had as its focus the restriction of the prerogative of the crown, thus, the restriction of sovereignty. In the 19th century, with the advent of popular sovereignty, there developed a renewed struggle between constitutionalism and absolutism, this time to restrict the sovereignty of the people. It is a struggle which is still being waged.

The focus is "social justice," over against a supposedly egotistical, unfair "market order," which in fact is the order of universal, integrating common law. It was precisely the pursuit of such "fairness" that, as we have seen, triggered the credit crisis of the late 2000s. The common law is under attack, the means of attack is legislation, and the rationale is provided by economics.

"This becomes evident when we examine the reason regularly given by the lawyers for the great changes that the character of law has undergone during the last hundred years," argues Hayek. "Everywhere, whether it be in English or American, French or German legal literature, we find alleged economic necessities given as the reasons for these changes. To the economist, reading the account by which the lawyers explain that transformation of the law, is a somewhat melancholy experience: he finds all the sins of his predecessors visited upon him."[135]

---

[135]Hayek, *Law, Legislation, and Liberty: Vol. 1*, p. 68.

Economics early on turned from extolling the virtues of the free market to cataloguing its sins. Free-market economic theory as it then existed did not help matters, for it insisted on presenting man as *homo economicus*, a rationalizing, self-seeking creature incessantly engaged in maximizing his own benefit regardless of the effect on others. Adam Smith's famous argument: "It is not from the benevolence of the butcher, the brewer, or the baker, that we expect our dinner, but from their regard to their own interest. We address ourselves, not to their humanity but to their self-love, and never talk to them of our own necessities but of their advantages" (*Wealth of Nations*, vol. I, ch. ii, sec. 2) was turned against him, as the economists of social welfare argued the soullessness of the market and the need for government to intervene to rectify its inequities and injustices.

As Hayek notes, it is this argument, referred to as the *social question*, that has legitimized all of the interventions in the functioning of *jurisdictio*, the private-legal order, on the part of government.

> [Such] accounts invariably speak of a past *laissez-faire* period, as if there had been a time when no efforts were made to improve the legal framework so as to make the market operate more beneficially or to supplement its results. Almost without exception they base their argument on the *fable convenue* that free enterprise has operated to the disadvantage of the manual workers, and allege that 'early capitalism' or 'liberalism' had brought about a decline in the material standard of the working class. The legend, although wholly untrue, has become part of the folklore of our time.[136]

---

[136] *Ibid.*

The agenda had already become clear in the period of the French Revolution, in the 1796 conspiracy led by François-Noël Babeuf to replace the Directory with a regime installing common property. It was also the driving force behind William Godwin's *Enquiry Concerning Political Justice* (first edition 1793) proclaiming the perfectibility of man precisely through the elimination of institutions such as property. And, of course, Jean-Jacques Rousseau ("The first man who enclosed a plot of ground and thought of saying, 'This is mine,' and found others stupid enough to believe him, was the true founder of civil society"[137]) was the *font et origo* hereof.

The social question concerned not the creation of wealth but its distribution. Wealth was distributed unequally, this was evident to all; that this unequal distribution was likewise inequitable, was the conviction of increasingly many. Given the ebbing conviction that human misery might have some link to human depravity – something any Augustinian Christian would have been quick to point out – another root of the problem had to be discovered, and it was promptly found in property and the other institutions of civil society. Godwin, for example, attributed "almost all the vices and misery that are seen in civil society to human institutions. Political regulations, and the established administration of property, are with him the fruitful sources of all evil, the hotbeds of all the crimes that degrade mankind."[138]

That an Augustinian voice was not entirely missing in the debates of the age is evident from the continuation

---

[137]Rousseau, *Discourse on Inequality,* in *The Basic Political Writings,* trans. Donald A. Cress (Indianapolis, Indiana: Hackett Publishing Company, 1987), p. 127.

[138]Malthus, *An Essay on the Principle of Population,* chap. 10, paragraph 4.

of the just-cited quotation: "But the truth is, that though human institutions appear to be the obvious and obtrusive causes of much mischief to mankind; yet, in reality, they are light and superficial, they are mere feathers that float on the surface, in comparison with those deeper seated causes of impurity that corrupt the springs, and render turbid the whole stream of human life." But, equally, that such a voice would garner mainly scorn and obloquy is evidence of the prejudice of the modern age, down through our day. For the writer was Thomas Robert Malthus; and if anyone has been vilified, or at the very least gravely misconstrued – after all, economics was supposedly dubbed "the dismal science" by Thomas Carlyle in response to Malthus' doctrine[139] – it is him, the contriver of so-called "Malthusianism," an epithet which speaks more of the prejudice of his opponents than of his own position.

Malthus dared to point out that the source of the misery in the world was not institutions but human nature itself. Human beings, led by passions and desires, have an inveterate propensity to engage in counterproductive behavior; the belief that reason could counteract that propensity was a pipe dream.

> The cravings of hunger, the love of liquor, the desire of possessing a beautiful woman, will urge men to actions, of the fatal consequences of which, to the general interests of society, they are perfectly well convinced, even at the very time

---

[139]The truth of the matter is, although Carlyle did refer to Malthus' treatment as "mournful... dreary, stolid, dismal, without hope for this world or the next," he did not refer to it as "the dismal science." For details see Robert Dixon, "The Origin of the Term 'Dismal Science' to Describe Economics," available on the World Wide Web at http://www.economics. unimelb. edu. au/ Tldevelopment/ econochat/ Dixonecon00.HTML.

they commit them. Remove their bodily cravings, and they would not hesitate a moment in determining against such actions. Ask them their opinion of the same conduct in another person, and they would immediately reprobate it.[140]

A universal propensity, this; its specific manifestation with the greatest effect on society is population growth. Now Malthus has been impugned and misrepresented regarding "Malthusianism" ever since he first put forward the argument. But what was that argument? It is - often represented in simplistic terms: 1) human beings are capable of reproducing at an exponential rate; 2) the means of subsistence can only be increased at an arithmetic rate; 3) therefore, population growth will always outstrip the means of subsistence.

But this is not precisely what Malthus said; and it certainly is not what he was getting at. What he said was that population growth, *if left unchecked,* would multiply at an exponential rate, thus outstripping the means of subsistence. But, one way or another, population growth *is* checked. It is a matter either of implementing desirable checks, or of being left at the mercy of undesirable checks, such as war, famine, and pestilence. And the whole point of Malthus' argument was to respond to Godwin's critique of civil society as being the source of society's problems. For Malthus' point was precisely to defend the institutions of civil society, specifically the family and private property, as *desirable* checks on what otherwise would be a miserable existence.

It seems highly probable, therefore, that an ad-

---

[140]Malthus, *An Essay on the Principle of Population*, chap. 13, paragraph 3.

ministration of property, not very different from
that which prevails in civilized States at present,
would be established, as the best, though inadequate, remedy, for the evils which were pressing
on the society.[141]

The institution of marriage, or at least, of some
express or implied obligation on every man to
support his own children, seems to be the natural
result of these reasonings in a community under -
the difficulties that we have supposed.[142]

But even given these institutions, a *moral* check is required above and beyond them. And this is the point to
which Malthus' argument was really leading: the need to
convince young people not to marry before they could
afford to support a family. Because marriage, family, and
property are no final solution, only indispensable means
thereto.

When these two fundamental laws of society, the
security of property, and the institution of marriage, were once established, inequality of conditions must necessarily follow. Those who were
born after the division of property, would come
into a world already possessed. If their parents,
from having too large a family, could not give
them sufficient for their support, what are they to
do in a world where every thing is appropri-
ated?[143]

---

[141]Malthus, *An Essay on the Principle of Population,* chap. 10,
paragraph 24.

[142]Malthus, *An Essay on the Principle of Population,* chap. 10,
paragraph 26.

[143]Malthus, *An Essay on the Principle of Population,* chap. 10,
paragraph 29.

And here Malthus laid his finger on the core of the issue. Institutions were important, extremely important, but they could not provide an ultimate solution. Ultimately, the solution comes in the form of personal accountability, of each individual making decisions and taking responsibility for those decisions. There could be no alleviation of the problem of poverty outside of this acceptance of personal accountability; but the notion that the root of the problem lies in institutions apart from personal accountability works precisely to perpetuate the problem.

This brings us back to the social question, which at bottom is not a question at all, but the inevitable result when society refuses to recognize the intrinsically moral character of the problem. Western societies faced then, and the "global community" faces today, the problem of an explosion of poverty wherein the population of the working class expands beyond the capacity of the labor market to employ it and for which inadequate infrastructure is in place to support the weight of numbers. The social question is the result when the real question – the question of character and morals – is left unanswered, and the resort is made to political solutions.

Case in point: England's poor laws ostensibly were introduced in order to stem the tide of poverty, but they had only made the problem worse. "It is a subject often started in conversation and mentioned always as a matter of great surprise," Malthus observed, "that notwithstanding the immense sum that is annually collected for the poor in England, there is still so much distress among them. Some think that the money must be embezzled; others that the church-wardens and overseers consume the greater part of it in dinners. All agree that somehow or other it must be very ill-managed. In short the fact, that nearly three millions are collected annually for the poor and yet that their distresses are not removed, is the subject of continual astonishment."[144] For Malthus, however, the problem was straightforward. The more money spent in such a manner to alleviate the condition of the poor, the more the problem would spread. And for good reason:

> I feel no doubt whatever that the parish laws of England have contributed to raise the price of provisions, and to lower the real price of labour. They have therefore contributed to impoverish that class of people whose only possession is their labour. It is also difficult to suppose that they have not powerfully contributed to generate that carelessness, and want of frugality observable among the poor, so contrary to the disposition frequently to be remarked among petty tradesmen and small farmers. The labouring poor, to use a vulgar expression, seem always to live from hand to mouth. Their present wants employ their whole attention, and they seldom think of the future. Even when they have an opportunity of saving they seldom exercise it; but all that is beyond their present necessities goes, generally speaking, to the ale-house. The poor-laws of England may therefore be said to diminish both the power and the will to save, among the common people, and thus to weaken one of the strongest incentives to sobriety and industry, and consequently to happiness.[145]

Far from being part of the solution, the poor laws were part of the problem. For by providing support to poor

---

[144]Malthus, *An Essay on the Principle of Population,* chap. 5, paragraph 3.

[145]Malthus, *An Essay on the Principle of Population,* chap. 5, paragraph 14.

families, these laws were simply encouraging their multiplication, thus leading to the "Malthusian" scenario.

Of course, this message was as ill-received as were the rest of Malthus' conclusions. The age simply did not want to hear of responsibility and accountability, much less of human depravity. But Malthus' message did find fertile soil in the imagination of the remarkable Thomas Chalmers, the noteworthy Scottish divine who translated Malthus' conclusions into an apology for the Christian state.

Chalmers' rejection of the welfare-state approach to poverty was decisive: "Pauperism in so far as sustained on the principle that each man, simply because he exists, holds a right on other men or on society for existence, is a thing not to be regulated but destroyed."[146] Nothing regarding this matter could be accomplished if its essentially moral character was not recognized. And coerced charity, the "charity of law," only made the matter intractable.

In the final chapter of his treatise on political economy, Chalmers sums up his discussion:

> We have laboured to demonstrate the futility of every expedient, which a mere political economy can suggest for the permanent well-being of a community. At best, they but tend to enlarge the absolute wealth of a country, without enlarging the relative comfort of the people who live in it. They may conduct to a larger, but not, on that account, to a happier society. They may tell on the condition of families, during those brief and evanescent seasons, when the population is somewhat in rear of the wealth; but, on the moment that this distance is overtaken, there will be the same straitness and discomfort as before....

---

[146]Chalmers, *Problems of Poverty*, p. 202.

There may be gleams of prosperity during the
fluctuations, or the few short and successive
stretches of enlargement which are yet in reserve
for us. But all around, and in every possible direction, there is a besetting limit, which the mighty
tide of an advancing population tends to over-
pass, and which, being impassible, throws the tide
back again upon general society; charged, as it
were, with a distress and a disorder that are exten-
sively felt throughout the old countries of the civilized world.[147]

Political economy alone is insufficient to rectify the
situation. Character is the key. "The high road, then, to a
stable sufficiency and comfort among the people, is
through the medium of their character; and this effectuated
by other lessons altogether than those of political economy." Economic science, though a fine thing in its proper
place, is powerless here. It is lessons of a moral nature
which are needed.

The moving force, that is to advance the general
multitude to a better and higher condition than
they now occupy, will not be brought to bear
upon them by the demonstrations, however just,
of any theory; and, in fact, the right impulse, and
the right habit, have often been exemplified, and
by large classes of peasantry, before the theory of
population was ever heard of. It is so in Norway;
and, most assuredly, without any inoculation of
principle from the school of Malthus. It was so in
Scotland, long before the promulgation of his
doctrines. In both countries, they realized, in
practice, what, in system and philosophy, they did
not understand. A moral and intelligent peasantry,

---

[147]Chalmers, *On Political Economy*, pp. 420-421.

imbued with a taste for the respectabilities of life, mixing prudence and foresight with every great practical step in the history of their doings, holding it discreditable to enter upon marriage without the likelihood of provision for a family – such a peasantry have more than once been exhibited in the annals of world, and may be made to re-appear.[148]

Now the fountain of such character is Christianity, which, in its zeal to realize a heavenly harvest of souls for eternity, preaches a doctrine which in its secondary effects produces precisely the sort of character which alleviates the problems signaled, but left unresolved, by political economy. "It is forgotten, that a warm and earnest Christianity, was the animating spirit of all our peculiar institutions, for generations after they were framed; and that, wanting this, they can no more perform the function of moralizing the people, than skeletons can perform the function or put forth the faculties of living men." The public schools as part of the church establishment imbued the populace with these salutary doctrines. "The scholastic is incorporated with the ecclesiastical system of Scotland; and that, not for the purposes of intolerance and exclusion, but for the purpose of sanctifying education, and plying the boyhood of our land with the lessons of the Bible. The scholarship of mere letters, might, to a certain extent have diffused intelligence amongst the people; but, it is mainly to the presence and power of the religious ingredient, that the moral greatness of our peasantry is owing."[149]

The social question could not be effectively answered through the mechanical means of political mea-

---

[148]Chalmers, *On Political Economy*, p. 422.
[149]Chalmers, *On Political Economy*, p. 434.

sures; yet this was the course men of influence were determined to take. "It would seem to argue a growing sense of
desperation among our public men, that their schemes of
patriotism and philanthropy are so thickening of late upon
us; while, but a semblance of relief, or, at the best, a
short-lived respite will be all the result of them." A fool's
errand; for "it is by the efficacy of moral means, working a
moral transformation, and by that alone, that our deliver-
ance will be effected; and little do the mere advocates of
retrenchment, and colonization, and public works, and
poor-laws, and other merely political expedients for the
melioration of the people – little do they know, how ut-
terly powerless all these enterprises are, while the Christianity of the land is unprovided for, and its Christian institutions are left inoperative, from the want of zealous and
energetic labourers to fill them."[150]

And this recalcitrance regarding Christianity's role
in society is likely attributable to deeper motives than mere
ignorance. "We fear, that with many [politicians and political economists], it may be distaste and antipathy." For they
cannot abide a living faith. "There is a certain style of
Christianity, a lifeless, inert, and meagre style of it, which is
tolerated in general society. But when it comes to be
Christianity in earnest, the Christianity that speaketh ur-
gently and importunately to the consciences of men, the
uncompromising Christianity that enjoins the holiness of
the New Testament in all its spirituality and extent, and
asserts the doctrine of the New Testament in all its depth
and all its peculiarity; such a Christianity has been very
generally denounced as fanaticism; and its faithful evangel-
ical expounders, have very generally had a stigma affixed to
them, and been outcasts from the patronage of the state."
From a spiritual standpoint, this is of course deplorable;

---

[150]Chalmers, *On Political Economy*, pp. 438-439.

but even from a prudential standpoint it is unwise. For – "this is the only Christianity that will either attract or moralize the population; and that, not because of its deceitful adaptation to vulgar prejudices, but, because of its truly divine adaptation to the actual workings of the human mind, and the felt necessities of human nature."[151]

If the political leadership insists on excising Christianity from its proper role in social life, it will call down a judgement upon the nation. "While this enmity to the truth as it is in Jesus operates in the hearts of our rulers, it is perhaps a vain expectation, that the civil and political importance of its being sounded forth from the pulpits of our land shall come to be recognised by them. On this subject, they may have been struck with judicial blindness; and ere Christianity shall manifest its power to regenerate our social condition, and overspread the land with prosperous and contented families; perhaps it will first vindicate itself on our ungodly nation, in the utter dissolution of an economy which disowns it, in the vengeance of some fearful overthrow."[152]

One thing was certain: no progress was possible if the "charity of law," the coercion of a misnamed charity, was allowed to take root. And here Chalmers writes a passage so prophetic of the future of Christianity that I include it in its entirety as an appendix.[153]

At its root was precisely confusion – willful confusion – regarding the very nature of justice. "We have long thought that by a legal provision for indigence, two principles of our moral nature have been confounded, which are radically distinct from each other.... These two principles are humanity and justice, whereof the latter is the only

---

[151]Chalmers, *On Political Economy,* pp. 439-440.

[152]Chalmers, *On Political Economy,* p. 440.

[153]See Appendix I, p. 117.

proper object of legislation – which, by attempting the enforcement of the former, has overstepped altogether its own rightful boundaries."[154] This confusion regarding justice had led to the situation in which the alleviation of poverty is accomplished not through charity or self-help, but as a matter of right by which one simply may claim the shortfall from society at large.

> Whatever the calls be, which the poverty of a human being may have on the compassion of his fellows – it has no claims whatever upon their justice. The confusion of these two virtues in the ethical system will tend to actual confusion and disorder, when introduced in the laws and administrations of human society. The proper remedy, or remedy of nature, for the wretchedness of the few, is the kindness of the many. But when the heterogeneous imagination of a right is introduced in to this department of human affairs, and the imagination is sanctioned by the laws of the country, then one of two things must follow – Either an indefinite encroachment on property, so as ultimately to reduce to a sort of agrarian level all the families of the land; or, if to postpone this consequence a rigid dispensation be adopted, the disappointment of a people who have been taught to feel themselves aggrieved, the innumerable heart-burnings which law itself has conjured up, and no administration of that law, however skilful, can appease.[155]

It is the entitlement mentality, the fruit of an alleged natural right to sustenance and provision, that is the result. It is the ultimate destruction of character and citizenship,

---

[154]*Problems of Poverty*, p. 201.
[155]*Problems of Poverty*, pp. 202-203.

and paves the way to slavery and dependence. We may remark in passing that the philosophy of natural rights hereby reaches its logical conclusion.

8. The Quest for Atonement

Malthus recognized the infernal influence set into motion by false charity. Chalmers recognized the falsehood of coercive charity, and the religious root of the social question. Yet neither of these divines penetrated to the core issue, which at bottom explains the anti-capitalist mentality[156] and the drive to expand government at the expense of the private sector. The underlying motivation is religious, and must be understood theologically.

Recall the discussion above, concerning the original human condition as being one of monolithic, mutually antagonistic groups (p. 53). Hayek also refers to this condition, but he does so from his evolutionary perspective, viewing purpose-oriented, group-oriented tribalism as mankind's original condition, with instincts to match, the remains of which linger in modern man as a subliminal consciousness, capable of rising to the surface when triggered or appealed to. His is a useful heuristic approach, even if his evolutionary methodology is not shared.[157]

Monolithic group life is superseded in the transition to a pluralistic order, one based in obedience to rules rather than commands – the civil condition. Such was not accomplished without trouble, as Hayek makes clear: "The

---

[156]Ludwig von Mises, *The Anti-Capitalistic Mentality* (Grove City, PA: Libertarian Press, 1972 [1956]).

[157]*Law, Legislation, and Liberty: Vol. 2: The Mirage of Social Justice*, ch. 11, "The Discipline of Abstract Rules and the Emotions of the Tribal Society."

rise of the ideal of impersonal justice based on formal rules has been achieved in a continuous struggle against those feelings of personal loyalty which provide the basis of the tribal society but which in the Great Society must not be allowed to influence the use of the coercive powers of government." The demotion of purpose and the supersession of the friend-foe relation enabled the establishment of a common life. "The gradual extension of a common order of peace from the small group to ever larger communities has involved constant clashes between the demands of sectional justice based on common visible purposes and the requirements of a universal justice equally applicable to the stranger and to the member of the group."[158]

The emotivism characteristic of contemporary politics has its roots in this existential condition. The transition from primitivism to civilization has left an original attachment to the primitive condition, a deep-seated well of emotion, based on a restricted, distributionist conception of justice. "This has caused a constant conflict between emotions deeply ingrained in human nature through millennia of tribal existence and the demands of abstract principles whose significance nobody fully grasped. Human emotions are attached to concrete objects, and the emotions of justice in particular are still very much connected with the visible needs of the group to which each person belongs." This mentality is incompatible with the universal, common-law order, the superiority, indeed necessity, of which is not readily apparent. "Only a mental reconstruction of the overall order of the Great Society enables us to comprehend that the deliberate aim at concrete common purposes, which to most people still appears as more meritorious and superior to blind obedience to abstract rules, would destroy that larger order in which all human

---

[158]*Law, Legislation, and Liberty: Vol. 2*, p. 143.

beings count alike." Peace is only possible when obligatory purpose is relegated to the level of voluntary participation. "It is only by extending the rules of just conduct to the relations with all other men, and at the same time depriving of their obligatory character those rules which cannot be universally applied, that we can approach a universal order of peace which might integrate all mankind into a single society." General rules, not purposive direction, are what integrate citizens into a common social order.[159]

What, then, is it about the civil condition that inspires so much resistance? For it cannot be denied that such resistance seems to multiply under conditions of obvious prosperity and progress. Is it simply a yearning for all-embracing, all-providing community that underlies this dissatisfaction?

There are various explanations to be given. One of the most convincing is provided by Helmut Schoeck in his important book, *Envy: A Theory of Social Behaviour.*[160] Schoeck traces the influence of envy in human society, from primitive cultures to modern democracies. He finds in envy a universal phenomenon of decisive influence in group behavior and in politics. It is a major reason that backward economies cannot advance; for individual effort yielding prosperity is viewed as intrinsically unjust and a violation of a preordained order. Conversely, economic progress has been accomplished in no small degree through the conquest of envy. "Most of the achievements which distinguish members of modern, highly developed and diversified societies from members of primitive societies – the development of civilization, in short – are the result of innumerable defeats inflicted on envy... and what Marxists have called the opiate of religion, the ability to

---

[159]*Law, Legislation, and Liberty: Vol. 2*, pp. 143-144.
[160]London: Secker & Warburg, 1966.

provide hope and happiness for believers in widely differing material circumstances, is nothing more than the provision of ideas which liberate the envious person from envy, the person envied from his sense of guilt and his fear of the envious."[161]

What Schoeck has uncovered here is the fundamental importance of the human heart to the social order. Envy is not a mere emotion, but a power capable of breaking the social order, or keeping it from advancing. But what he does not sufficiently appreciate is the basis of envy in guilt.

Schoeck sees in guilt a *response* of the *envied* person, of the successful and prosperous, to being envied. "The condition of anxiety, the feeling of guilt, the fear of a retributive catastrophe (Polycrates' ring) — all this is a combination of superstition and empirically verifiable (i.e., realistic) anxiety about another person's — usually a neighbour's — envy."[162] In Western society, Christianity has overcome this penchant. "As long as the Christian (or at least the man still partially imbued with Christian culture) in his attitude to his fellow men still intuitively models his conduct on a supernatural exemplar, the potential innovator's neighbour, fellow villager or colleague will, in ideal circumstances (reality being often in default), represent less of an inhibition or threat than would have been the case in the pre- or non-Christian world."[163] And the influence of Christianity in this has lasted even into the age of secularism: "agnostic and atheistic societies, as well as states and regimes, have profited by the opportunity for individual achievement made possible by Christianity, because they have often developed a system of incentives which re-

---

[161]Schoeck, *Envy*, p. 2.

[162]Schoeck, *Envy*, p. 126.

[163]Schoeck, *Envy*, p. 127.

wards the individual extravagantly but is tolerable to him only because he feels in some measure secure against the envy of his companions – thanks to the persistence, albeit in diluted form, of Christian values."[164]

But guilt is more than just a response to envy. Rather, it can also accompany envy, or rather, envy can accompany guilt; guilt, then, gives rise to envy. The guilty person is also the person who owes something to someone else, and the very fact of being obligated generates the envy which then fastens onto any object of supposedly better fortune.

We have arrived at a very important point in the discussion: the enmity engendered in the civil condition is brought about by the obligation upon which the civil condition is based. Obligation is guilt. Guilt is not the guilt of fault only, but the guilt of debt. It is no coincidence that Germanic languages, such as German and Dutch, use the same word, schuld, for guilt and for debt.[165] At bottom, they both refer to something owed, something outstanding which has to be rectified. The civil condition is based on the expansion of this form of obligation. The jural relations of private law revolve around obligation. Obligation is what enables the pluralist, associationalist social order to arise. It is a major reason for communication.

A huge literature has been engendered over the years highlighting the connection between the capitalist order on the one hand and alienation, anomie, all manner of guilt – class guilt, race guilt, Third-World guilt – on the other. The two seem to go together. There never seems to be a reconciliation between the achievements of an advancing society, on the one hand, and its aspirations, on

---

[164]*Ibid.*

[165]Similarly, New Testament Greek uses the same root word for sins, offences, debts, and guilt: οφειλω; see, e.g., Matthew 6:12.

the other. And that not least because the aspirations may be contradictory: for further advance and progress, on the one hand, and for a return to a simpler age, on the other.

The socialist psychologist Erich Fromm is one of the many to have given eloquent expression to these contradictions. His essay, "The Present Human Condition,"[166] provides a succinct example, striking in its ability to hit the mark and yet miss it at the same time. "What kind of man, then, does our society need in order to function smoothly? It needs men who co-operate easily in large groups, who want to consume more and more, and whose tastes are standardized and can be easily influenced and anticipated. It needs men who feel free and independent, not subject to any authority or principle or conscience, yet are willing to be commanded, to do what is expected, to fit into the social machine without friction; men who can be guided without force, led without leaders, be prompted without an aim, except the aim to be on the move, to function, to go ahead." Fromm has accurately captured contemporary democratic man, suffused with the conviction that he is his own man and the master of his own destiny, all the while being led by the nose by powers of which he is not entirely aware. But then comes the obligatory theme of alienation: "This kind of man, modern industrialism has succeeded in producing; he is the automaton, the alienated man. He is alienated, in the sense that his actions and his own forces have become estranged from him; they stand above him and against him, and rule him rather than being ruled by him. His life forces have been transformed into things and institutions; and these things and institutions have become idols. They are experienced not as the result of man's own efforts but as something apart from him, which he wor-

---

[166]In *The Dogma of Christ and Other Essays on Religion, Psychology and Culture* (New York: Holt, Rinehart and Winston, 1963).

ships and to which he submits."[167]

Fromm here hits upon the same theme that Hayek does, to wit, that pluralistic, multi-associational, multi-goal-oriented civil society removes an immediate ultimacy from the individual's activity so that in his activity he may lose touch with a sense of purpose. But this, in Hayek's view, is not anything to regret, but rather to embrace; for it is the precondition of freedom. "While in the tribal society the condition of internal peace is the devotion of all members to some common visible purposes, and therefore to the will of somebody who can decide what at any moment these purposes are to be and how they are to be achieved, the Open Society of free men becomes possible only when the individuals are constrained only to obey the abstract rules that demarcate the domain of the means that each is allowed to use for his purposes."[168] As Oakeshott emphasizes, an overall purpose is eschewed; there is only agreement to obey rules.[169]

---

[167]Fromm, *The Dogma of Christ*, pp. 97-98.

[168]Hayek, *Law, Legislation, and Liberty: Vol. 2*, p. 144.

[169]"Thus, *respublica* [i.e., "republic"] does not define or even describe a common substantive purpose, interest, or 'good'. It cannot itself be an object of want, although where it has to be defended against dissolution or destruction it may temporarily and equivocally become an agreed common want, as mere 'survival' may become a want but only in circumstances of threatened extinction. It is not a suppositious sum of all approved purposes, a purpose which remains when all competing purposes have cancelled one another, or one which represents a consensus or harmony of purposes from which discordant purposes have been excluded, or one upon which all or a majority of associates are agreed, or any other such imagined, wished-for and sought-after substantive condition of things. Nor is it a 'policy' composed of 'managerial' decisions and constituting a strategy or a tactic in terms of which a common purpose might be contingently pursued. It is not a schedule of awards of advantage or disadvantage to interests or a scheme for the distribution of the burdens of being associated. On the contrary, it is a manifold of rules and rule-like prescriptions to be subscribed

Civil society "requir[es] a predominance of abstract rational principles over those emotions that are evoked by the particular and the concrete, or the predominance of conclusions derived from abstract rules, whose significance was little understood, over the spontaneous response to the perception of concrete effects which touched the lives and conditions of those familiar to us." Associational life is transformed; its purposiveness is dethroned from ultimacy to multiplicity, and so, therefore, is its authority. Morality becomes distinct from law. "Since in a society of free men the membership in such special groups will be voluntary, there must also be no power of enforcing the rules of such groups. It is in such a free society that a clear distinction between the moral rules which are not enforced and the rules of law which are enforced becomes so important. If the smaller groups are to be integrated into the more comprehensive order of society at large, it must be through the free movement of individuals between groups into which they may be accepted if they submit to their rules."[170]

It is, thus, a lack of maturity and an inability fully to accept the prerequisites of civil society that leads to alienation, not any intrinsic shortcoming of civil society itself. "The revolt against the abstractness of the rules we are required to obey in the Great Society [i.e., civil society], and the predilection for the concrete which we feel to be human, are thus merely a sign that intellectually and morally we have not yet fully matured to the needs of the impersonal comprehensive order of mankind."[171]

---

to in all the enterprises and adventures in which the self-chosen satisfactions of agents may be sought." Oakeshott, *On Human Conduct*, pp. 147-148.

[170]Hayek, *Law, Legislation, and Liberty: Vol. 2*, pp. 148-149.

[171]Hayek, *Law, Legislation, and Liberty: Vol. 2*, p. 149.

In his discussion, Fromm then makes the crucial observation that modern man turns to the state to compensate for the lack of purpose and community he perceives in civil society. "Man's social feelings are projected into the state. As a citizen he is willing even to give his life for his fellow men; as a *private* individual he is governed by egotistical concern with himself. Because he has made the state the embodiment of his own social feelings, he worships it and its symbols. He projects his sense of power, wisdom, and courage into his leaders, and he worships these leaders as his idols."[172]

And this transference of religious devotion to the state comes in tandem with a relaxation of the Christianity which helped give birth to the Western order of liberty. "We claim that we pursue the aims of the Judaeo-Christian tradition: the love of God and of our neighbor. We are even told that we are going through a period of a promising religious renaissance. Nothing could be further from the truth. We use symbols belonging to a genuinely religious tradition and transform them into formulas serving the purpose of alienated man. Religion has become an empty shell; it has been transformed into a self-help device for increasing one's own powers for success. God becomes a partner in business. *The Power of Positive Thinking* is the successor of *How to Win Friends and Influence People*."[173]

The state, then, is the new idol. It is the vehicle to overcome the inherent lack of community in civil society. But behind this lack of community lurks the ever-present mutual commitment and obligation of which civil society is composed. These come to be seen as obstacles, hindrances, obstructions to true community. Hence, behind the perceived lack of community is the revolt against obli-

---

[172]Fromm, *The Dogma of Christ*, p. 98.
[173]Fromm, *The Dogma of Christ*, p. 100.

gation. And underlying this revolt is man's existential condition as a sinful creature, guilty before God and alienated from Him, and thus in eternal debt to Him. This ultimate, cosmic alienation and guilt is what all other obligation points to, and reminds of. Obligation is the human condition; it is the result of the primordial revolt; and it is a standing affront to rebellious man.

This existential condition of man was dealt with conclusively by Western Christianity. That which sets Western Christianity apart – and which, in fact, enabled the growth of the common-law social orders of Western civilization – is judicial theology. Such a theology, already anticipated by Augustine, was given explicit, albeit provisional, shape by Anselm, Archbishop of Canterbury.[174] In his dialogue *Cur Deus Homo,* "Why God Became Man," Anselm laid out the structure of justice in such a way as to explain the necessity of obligation and the achievement of its ultimate extinguishment.

In Christ, God became man. He did so in order to satisfy, through His atoning work on the cross, the claim of justice, by paying for man's sins; and so He restored community, by extending that payment to man so as to redeem him to relationship with the Father.

This atonement therefore is crucial not simply to the salvation of one's soul, but to the very existence of civil society. It is what enabled the transition to a full-fledged civil society. This atonement separates guilt and debt by separating atonement from the administration of justice. Atonement is achieved once and for all through the work of Christ on the cross; the church administers

---

[174]See Stahl's discussion of justice and the atonement in §§. 56-59, Volume II, Book I of his *Philosophy of Law,* a translation of which is scheduled for publication in 2010. Stahl takes Anselm's discussion of the atonement forward; the following discussion is based on his seminal statement.

the sacrament of Holy Supper as the celebration of that work. Thus atonement is removed from the repertoire of the organized political society, leaving the administration of justice and the capacity to enforce the regime of private law in the hands of the state. And this liberation, brought about by the Augustinian separation of church and state, allowed the civilization of capitalism to be engendered.

The "guilt" that capitalism engenders, debt, fuels the drive for atonement which underlies the religious fanaticism all civilizations have exemplified. For consider that it was the most capitalistic societies of the ancient world, the Phoenician and Carthaginian, which also exhibited the most blatant and revolting forms of the quest for atonement: child sacrifice. The capacity to sustain capitalism can only be found in the ability to separate atonement from justice, guilt from debt. That is why capitalism is the product of the Augustinian West. And that is why it cannot be sustained if that civilization is allowed to be destroyed by multiculturalism, relativism, and a false doctrine of the neutrality of the state. For the "neutral" state, by abandoning the Augustinian distinctive, dismantles the separation of atonement and justice, and opens the door to the return of the politics of envy.

Atonement, then, made possible the administration of justice by the state, whereby the state restricts its activity primarily to the administration of justice. The *church* enabled it to do so, for by establishing its ministry of the restoration of community in the midst of the social order, the church called upon the state to leave off the task of coerced community to assume its proper task as "the minister of God, a revenger to execute wrath upon him that doeth evil" (Romans 13:4).

To some this may seem a grave overstatement. Surely the state can be called upon to administer justice in this manner without any appeal to the atoning work of

Christ – is this not the conviction of all who call for the "wall of separation" between church and state, who place their hope in the promise of the *neutral state?*

But this is precisely what is wrong with such neutral theories of the state, and the role of religion in society. *Justice cannot be achieved until atonement is achieved:* ancient societies perceived this, and made sacrifice – plant, animal, even human – an integral part of their public life. Modern man thinks he has escaped this necessity, relegating religion to the private sphere, secularizing the public square. This is pure self-deception.

Ancient societies instituted the most grotesque rituals – fertility rites, bloodstained child immolations, etc. – so as to lay the basis for common human life.[175] But Christianity realized the substance of that which other human societies perversely pursued. For Christ died on the cross, in a *public* execution, "that one man should die for the people, and that the whole nation perish not" as the high priest Caiaphas unwittingly prophesied (John 11:51), providing a full, common, public atonement (the crucifixion a "public display" of Christ's triumph: Colossians 2:15). In this, the quest for perfect justice is exposed as another manifestation of the attempt to "immanentize the eschaton," to use Voegelin's phrase, to realize the Day of Judgement here on earth by human hands. For Christ, "Whom the heaven must receive until the times of restitution of all things" (Acts 3:21), has removed that necessity, placing it in heaven where it belongs, until that time.

The atonement realized through Christ on the cross

---

[175]Heinsohn has brought this reality to light in his enlightening book *Der Erschaffung der Götter: Das Opfer als Ursprung der Religion* [The Creation of the Gods: Sacrifice as the Origin of Religion] (Reinbek bei Hamburg: Rowohlt, 1997). Although his conclusions are to this author unacceptable, his argument, that sacrifice laid the foundations for civilization, is well-taken.

is *satisfactio*, the perfect payment for the sins committed by man. Yet even more than this, it is the payment, beyond sins, of sin. Sin is the mysterious power which has man in its grip and which makes it impossible for him to please God. Sins had to be paid for, but the power of sin had also to be broken. This is the full meaning of atonement. Such a cosmic, trans-historical deed transcends every effort to punish sin and eradicate guilt in this world. It also obviates the need to do so. Henceforth, the state need no basis in an atonement of its own making; it can rest upon the atonement attained outside of it. This is what frees the state to pursue justice, while also restricting it to this pursuit.

Universal atonement is administered to the world through the church's ministry of mercy, exercised firstly through the ministry of Word and Sacrament. Through this ministry the church makes felt its jurisdiction; and in so doing it makes room for the jurisdiction of the state, and for the jurisdictions of a pluralistic social order. "And many people shall go and say, Come ye, and let us go up to the mountain of the LORD, to the house of the God of Jacob; and he will teach us of his ways, and we will walk in his paths: for out of Zion shall go forth the law, and the word of the LORD from Jerusalem" (Micah 4:2). So the common law is rooted in common atonement, resulting in the positive legal orders of the community of free nations.

Where this atonement is not acknowledged, justice itself merges into atonement and cannot be distinguished from it. That is when atonement is *sought* through the administration of justice, rather than being received. Justice rests on atonement and cannot exist apart from it. Justice receives its full depth and breadth in human life when it flows from mercy as expressed in the atonement, not when it is severed therefrom, for then commences the ultimate confusion of justice and mercy, of law and grace, wherein the one consumes the other. It matters not which consumes which, the end result is the same.

The modern political apostasy began with the French Revolution – "Ni Dieu ni maître" – which, interestingly enough, chronologically accompanied the rise of the modern welfare state. Both were the fruit of the new philosophy of man whereby the individual becomes the source of law, the institutions of civil society the adventitious outworking, a shell to be shucked off at will. The result is the entitlement mentality, against which Thomas Chalmers expostulated with true righteous anger. It is also the warped mentality which has given us political correctness – the religious zeal to silence all conflicting opinions in the name of freedom of expression. The zeal of the Left can only be seen against the background of the loss of religion in public life; for its zeal is the zeal of the religious fanatic, aiming through the vehicle of the state and politics to achieve perfect justice and full atonement.

How else is one to explain the consuming desire to silence opposition and in fact eliminate it, which has characterized all collectivist movements? The National Socialists under Adolph Hitler certainly were not the only ones to practice this; in fact, in Germany they managed to triumph over socialists and communists pursuing equally vile ends through equally vile practices; it was merely a form of survival of the collectivist fittest. Josef Stalin, Mao Tse Tung, Fidel Castro, Saddam Hussein – all pursuing total power by root-and-branch elimination of the opposition, all equally feted by the Left. For it is power they are after, power which is required by their religion, a religion which requires total sacrifice, through which alone the coveted atonement can be attained.

This power, and this elimination of obligation, can only be achieved by eliminating the pluralist order of mutual obligation as contained in the jural relations of private law. All must be subsumed into a single, all-embracing community, eliminating all vestiges of obligation, debt, guilt – where all is one and one is all. And freedom will be dead.

9. Conclusion

For conservatives, the message is clear: the social order of natural rights has been a distinct failure. It has given us, in place of a robust common-law regime as a guarantee of liberty and restraint on government, the pottage of separation of powers, itself powerless in the face of the new sovereign, the people, and its unaccountable representatives. Absolute subjective right, which is what the natural rights philosophy boils down to, leads directly to the entitlement mentality, then the uncontrolled electorate, and finally to the justification of government intervention in the private sector in order to provide for all those rights, to achieve "fairness," the fabled will-o'-the wisp of "social justice."

What is more, the emphasis on natural rights is precisely what prompted the abandonment of confessional Christianity in public life, which has directly led to the political quest for atonement, the driving force behind anti-capitalism, and the ever-present threat of the overthrow of the pluralist social order.

We live in an age which seems to be ripe for comprehensive reforms. We hear calls for comprehensive immigration reform, comprehensive health-care reform, comprehensive school reform. It is time that conservatives came up with their own agenda for comprehensive reform: comprehensive *entitlement* reform. To tell the "sovereign people" that sovereignty does not extend to the overthrow of the rights of property and contract, to the overthrow by *gubernaculum* of *jurisdictio*. It is precisely the idea that citizens – and even non-citizens, as witness illegal aliens – are *not* entitled to the wealth their fellow citizens have created. As Chalmers so eloquently stated (and it bears repeating):

"Pauperism in so far as sustained on the principle that each man, simply because he exists, holds a right on other men or on society for existence, is a thing not to be regulated but destroyed."[176] It is the entitlement mentality which has driven the attack on the common law, the bastion of rights of property and contract. The common law must be recovered as an independent, integral order in its own right, embodying institutions and principles of justice which are sacrosanct and cannot be violated with impunity. Citizenship must be recovered as a sacred trust the bond of which is a commitment to uphold this order of law rather than subvert it through the political process, in favor of one's own interest.

The key to accomplishing this is to recover the understanding of liberty as inheritance rather than natural right. This means that liberty is grounded in the order of an unassailable legal framework. Liberty does not create the legal order, for that order's integrity stands above the manipulation of man, and its fundamental principles and institutions can only be received and implemented. Liberty as inheritance also means that there is nothing natural about the legal order: because it is an inheritance, it is to be received as a precious heirloom, an artifact of many generations' labor, not something that, in Ortega y Gasset's words, "*is there* in just the same way as the earth's crust and the forest primeval."[177] Leoni's admonition, in a slightly different context, must be taken to heart if conservatism is to restore its, and the nation's, foundations:

> A free market seems something more "natural" than government or at least independent of government, if not, indeed, something that it is neces-

---

[176]Chalmers, *Problems of Poverty*, p. 202.
[177]José Ortega y Gasset, *Revolt of the Masses*, p. 126.

sary to maintain "against" the government. In fact, a market is no more "natural" than government itself, and both are no more natural than, say, bridges. People who ignore this fact ought to take seriously a couplet once sung in a cabaret in Montmartre:

Voyez comme la nature a en un bon sens bien profond
À faire passer les fleuves justement sous les ponts.
(See how Nature had the extreme good sense
To make the rivers flow exactly under the bridges.)[178]

---

[178]Leoni, *Freedom and the Law*, p. 50.

Appendix I:
Chalmers on the
Entitlement Mentality

This excerpt from Thomas Chalmers' *On Political Economy* speaks volumes about the roots of the secularization of society precisely in the instrumentality of the welfare state. The entitlement mentality it fosters is fundamentally at odds with the Christian faith and the character that faith fosters. To wit —

"5. But we must here remark, that, for the purpose of a general economic improvement, to be brought about by the means of Christian education, a gradual abolition of the compulsory provision for indigence, which now obtains in England, and hangs menacingly over Ireland, seems to us indispensable. We can anticipate no rise of wages, no elevation in the state and sufficiency of the working classes, from any efforts to instruct and Christianize them, however strenuous, if the pauperism and the education are to go on contemporaneously. We, in the first place, feel quite assured, from the moral influences of this public charity, that it operates as a dead weight on the ministrations of the clergymen, aud stands most grievously in the way of their success. But, in the second place, however vigorous and effective his exertions may be, at the most, and while the present system of poor's laws continues, we shall have two distinct populations, each marked by opposite extremes of character. The clergyman, on the one hand, may reclaim hundreds to principle and sobriety who shall form a wholesome and better class of peasantry. But the parish vestry, on the other, remains an attractive nucleus, around which there will gather and settle, in every little district of the land, a depraved and improvident class, whom the temptation of this legal charity has called into being, and who will bid inveterate defiance to all the moral energy which might be brought to bear upon them. The very presence of such a class even though but a fraction of the community, will, with their reckless habits, depress and overbear the general condition of labourers. A very few supernumeraries, we have seen, will suffice for this effect. So that whether the temptation to improvidence operates on all the people, or only on part of them, still that redundancy is generated which tells so adversely on the general rate of wages, and so on the comfort and circumstances of the population at large. Education will make head against mendicity. It will make head against poverty in any other form than that fixed aud legalized, and invested with the challenging, as its right at the bar of justice, which should have been left to the willing sympathies of nature. But shielded and encouraged as it is in the parishes of England, it will stand its ground, against every attempt to dislodge it from those innumerable fastnesses which it now occupies; and in spite of every counteractive, whether by the Christian or literary education of the people, will it remain an incubus on the prosperity and comfort of the lower orders" (*On Political Economy*, pp. 429-432).

Can a better or more prophetic summary of the deleterious effects of the welfare state upon Christianity be imagined? Pauperism, or the entitlement mentality, has worked to undermine the church ever since it was introduced. And this is how it went about its work: by calling the poor away from sobriety and restraint to depravity and improvidence, from there gradually overbearing the entire population. Proper education, education in virtue, can overcome poverty but not pauperism. It is a telling statistic that the church's role in society, even its relative number of adherents, has plummeted during the entire regime of the welfare state. The entitlement mentality is at war with the Christian faith. The two are irreconcilable. It is not that the working classes have been turned into a group of criminals or some such thing that is the problem: it is the mentality whereby the government is looked to in the way God used to be looked to: it is, in a word, *idolatry*.

Appendix II: Burke on Natural Rights

From *Select Works of Edmund Burke*. A New Imprint of the Payne Edition. Foreword and Biographical Note by Francis Canavan (Indianapolis: Liberty Fund, 1999). Vol. 2.

The Revolution[179] was made to preserve our ancient, indisputable laws and liberties and that ancient constitution of government which is our only security for law and liberty. If you are desirous of knowing the spirit of our constitution and the policy which predominated in that great period which has secured it to this hour, pray look for both in our histories, in our records, in our acts of parliament, and journals of parliament, and not in the sermons of the Old Jewry and the after-dinner toasts of the Revolution Society. In the former you will find other ideas and another language. Such a claim is as ill-suited to our temper and wishes as it is unsupported by any appearance of authority. The very idea of the fabrication of a new government is enough to fill us with disgust and horror. We wished at the period of the Revolution, and do now wish, to derive all we possess as an inheritance from our forefathers. Upon that body and stock of inheritance we have taken care not to inoculate any cyon alien to the nature of

---

[179] A reference to the so-called "Glorious Revolution" of 1688 by which James Stuart was acknowledged to have abdicated the throne, in favor of William and Mary.

the original plant. All the reformations we have hitherto made have proceeded upon the principle of reverence to antiquity; and I hope, nay, I am persuaded, that all those which possibly may be made hereafter will be carefully formed upon analogical precedent, authority, and example.

Our oldest reformation is that of Magna Charta. You will see that Sir Edward Coke, that great oracle of our law, and indeed all the great men who follow him, to Blackstone, are industrious to prove the pedigree of our liberties. They endeavor to prove that the ancient charter, the Magna Charta of King John, was connected with another positive charter from Henry I, and that both the one and the other were nothing more than a reaffirmance of the still more ancient standing law of the kingdom. In the matter of fact, for the greater part these authors appear to be in the right; perhaps not always; but if the lawyers mistake in some particulars, it proves my position still the more strongly, because it demonstrates the powerful prepossession toward antiquity, with which the minds of all our lawyers and legislators, and of all the people whom they wish to influence, have been always filled, and the stationary policy of this kingdom in considering their most sacred rights and franchises as an inheritance.

In the famous law of the 3rd of Charles I, called the Petition of Right, the parliament says to the king, "Your subjects have inherited this freedom", claiming their franchises not on abstract principles "as the rights of men", but as the rights of Englishmen, and as a patrimony derived from their forefathers. Selden and the other profoundly learned men who drew this Petition of Right were as well acquainted, at least, with all the general theories concerning the "rights of men" as any of the discoursers in our pulpits or on your tribune; full as well as Dr. Price or as the Abbe Sieyes. But, for reasons worthy of that practical wisdom which superseded their theoretic science, they preferred this positive, recorded, hereditary title to all which can be dear to the man and the citizen, to that vague speculative right which exposed their sure inheritance to be scrambled for and torn to pieces by every wild, litigious spirit.

The same policy pervades all the laws which have since been made for the preservation of our liberties. In the 1st of William and Mary, in the famous statute called the Declaration of Right, the two Houses utter not a syllable of "a right to frame a government for themselves". You will see that their whole care was to secure the religion, laws, and liberties that had been long possessed, and had been lately endangered. "Taking into their most serious consideration the best means for making such an establishment, that their religion, laws, and liberties might not be in danger of being again subverted", they auspicate all their proceedings by stating as some of those best means, "in the first place" to do "as their ancestors in like cases have usually done for vindicating their ancient rights and liberties, to declare" – and then they pray the king and queen "that it may be declared and enacted that all and singular the rights and liberties asserted and declared are the true ancient and indubitable rights and liberties of the people of this kingdom".

You will observe that from Magna Charta to the Declaration of Right it has been the uniform policy of our constitution to claim and assert our liberties as an entailed inheritance derived to us from our forefathers, and to be transmitted to our posterity – as an estate specially belonging to the people of this kingdom, without any reference whatever to any other more general or prior right. By this means our constitution preserves a unity in so great a diversity of its parts. We have an inheritable crown, an inheritable peerage, and a House of Commons and a people inheriting privileges, franchises, and liberties from a long line of ancestors.

This policy appears to me to be the result of profound reflection, or rather the happy effect of following nature, which is wisdom without reflection, and above it. A spirit of innovation is generally the result of a selfish temper and confined views. People will not look forward to posterity, who never look backward to their ancestors. Besides, the people of England well know that the idea of inheritance furnishes a sure principle of conservation and a sure principle of transmission, without at all excluding a principle of improvement. It leaves acquisition free, but it secures what it acquires. Whatever advantages are obtained by a state proceeding on these maxims are locked fast as in a sort of family settlement, grasped as in a kind of mortmain forever. By a constitutional policy, working after the pattern of nature, we receive, we hold, we transmit our government and our privileges in the same manner in which we enjoy and transmit our property and our lives. The institutions of policy, the goods of fortune, the gifts of providence are handed down to us, and from us, in the same course and order. Our political system is placed in a just correspondence and symmetry with the order of the world and with the mode of existence decreed to a permanent body composed of transitory parts, wherein, by the disposition of a stupendous wisdom, molding together the great mysterious incorporation of the human race, the whole, at one time, is never old or middle-aged or young, but, in a condition of unchangeable constancy, moves on through the varied tenor of perpetual decay, fall, renovation, and progression. Thus, by preserving the method of nature in the conduct of the state, in what we improve we are never wholly new; in what we retain we are never wholly obsolete. By adhering in this manner and on those principles to our forefathers, we are guided not by the superstition of antiquarians, but by the spirit of philosophic analogy. In this choice of inheritance we have given to our frame of polity the image of a relation in blood, binding up the constitution of our country with our dearest domestic ties, adopting our fundamental laws into the bosom of our family affections, keeping inseparable and cherishing with the warmth of all their combined and mutually reflected charities our state, our hearths, our sepulchres, and our altars.

Through the same plan of a conformity to nature in our artificial institutions, and by calling in the aid of her unerring and powerful instincts to fortify the fallible and feeble contrivances of our reason, we have derived several other, and those no small, benefits from considering our liberties in the light of an inheritance. Always acting as if in the presence of canonized forefathers, the spirit of freedom, leading in itself to misrule and excess, is tempered with an awful gravity. This idea of a liberal descent inspires us with a sense of habitual native dignity which prevents that upstart insolence almost inevitably adhering to and disgracing those who are the first acquirers of any distinction. By this means our liberty becomes a noble freedom.

It carries an imposing and majestic aspect. It has a pedigree and illustrating ancestors. It has its bearings and its ensigns armorial. It has its gallery of portraits, its monumental inscriptions, its records, evidences, and titles. We procure reverence to our civil institutions on the principle upon which nature teaches us to revere individual men: on account of their age and on account of those from whom they are descended. All your sophisters cannot produce anything better adapted to preserve a rational and manly freedom than the course that we have pursued, who have chosen our nature rather than our speculations, our breasts rather than our inventions, for the great conservatories and magazines of our rights and privileges (37-41).

IT is no wonder, therefore, that with these ideas of

everything in their constitution and government at home, either in church or state, as illegitimate and usurped, or at best as a vain mockery, they look abroad with an eager and passionate enthusiasm. Whilst they are possessed by these notions, it is vain to talk to them of the practice of their ancestors, the fundamental laws of their country, the fixed form of a constitution whose merits are confirmed by the solid test of long experience and an increasing public strength and national prosperity. They despise experience as the wisdom of unlettered men; and as for the rest, they have wrought underground a mine that will blow up, at one grand explosion, all examples of antiquity, all precedents, charters, and acts of parliament. They have "the rights of men". Against these there can be no prescription, against these no agreement is binding; these admit no temperament and no compromise; anything withheld from their full demand is so much of fraud and injustice. Against these their rights of men let no government look for security in the length of its continuance, or in the justice and lenity of its administration. The objections of these speculatists, if its forms do not quadrate with their theories, are as valid against such an old and beneficent government as against the most violent tyranny or the greenest usurpation. They are always at issue with governments, not on a question of abuse, but a question of competency and a question of title. I have nothing to say to the clumsy subtilty of their political metaphysics. Let them be their amusement in the schools. — "Illa se jactet in aula Aeolus, et clauso ventorum carcere regnet". — But let them not break prison to burst like a Levanter to sweep the earth with their hurricane and to break up the fountains of the great deep to overwhelm us.

Far am I from denying in theory, full as far is my heart from withholding in practice (if I were of power to give or to withhold) the real rights of men. In denying their false claims of right, I do not mean to injure those which are real, and are such as their pretended rights would totally destroy. If civil society be made for the advantage of man, all the advantages for which it is made become his right. It is an institution of beneficence; and law itself is only beneficence acting by a rule. Men have a right to live by that rule; they have a right to do justice, as between their fellows, whether their fellows are in public function or in ordinary occupation. They have a right to the fruits of their industry and to the means of making their industry fruitful. They have a right to the acquisitions of their parents, to the nourishment and improvement of their offspring, to instruction in life, and to consolation in death. Whatever each man can separately do, without trespassing upon others, he has a right to do for himself; and he has a right to a fair portion of all which society, with all its combinations of skill and force, can do in his favor. In this partnership all men have equal rights, but not to equal things. He that has but five shillings in the partnership has as good a right to it as he that has five hundred pounds has to his larger proportion. But he has not a right to an equal dividend in the product of the joint stock; and as to the share of power, authority, and direction which each individual ought to have in the management of the state, that I must deny to be amongst the direct original rights of man in civil society; for I have in my contemplation the civil social man, and no other. It is a thing to be settled by convention.

If civil society be the offspring of convention, that convention must be its law. That convention must limit and modify all the descriptions of constitution which are formed under it. Every sort of legislative, judicial, or executory power are its creatures. They can have no being in any other state of things; and how can any man claim under the conventions of civil society rights which do not so

much as suppose its existence — rights which are absolutely repugnant to it? One of the first motives to civil society, and which becomes one of its fundamental rules, is
that no man should be judge in his own cause. By this
each person has at once divested himself of the first fundamental right of uncovenanted man, that is, to judge for
himself and to assert his own cause. He abdicates all right
to be his own governor. He inclusively, in a great measure,
abandons the right of self-defense, the first law of nature.
Men cannot enjoy the rights of an uncivil and of a civil
state together. That he may obtain justice, he gives up his
right of determining what it is in points the most essential
to him. That he may secure some liberty, he makes a sur-
render in trust of the whole of it.

Government is not made in virtue of natural rights,
which may and do exist in total independence of it, and
exist in much greater clearness and in a much greater degree of abstract perfection; but their abstract perfection is
their practical defect. By having a right to everything they
want everything. Government is a contrivance of human
wisdom to provide for human wants. Men have a right
that these wants should be provided for by this wisdom.
Among these wants is to be reckoned the want, out of civil
society, of a sufficient restraint upon their passions. Society requires not only that the passions of individuals
should be subjected, but that even in the mass and body,
as well as in the individuals, the inclinations of men should
frequently be thwarted, their will controlled, and their passions brought into subjection. This can only be done by a
power out of themselves, and not, in the exercise of its
function, subject to that will and to those passions which it
is its office to bridle and subdue. In this sense the re-
straints on men, as well as their liberties, are to be reckoned among their rights. But as the liberties and the re-
strictions vary with times and circumstances and admit to

infinite modifications, they cannot be settled upon any abstract rule; and nothing is so foolish as to discuss them upon that principle.

The moment you abate anything from the full rights of men, each to govern himself, and suffer any artificial, positive limitation upon those rights, from that moment the whole organization of government becomes a consideration of convenience. This it is which makes the constitution of a state and the due distribution of its powers a matter of the most delicate and complicated skill. It requires a deep knowledge of human nature and human necessities, and of the things which facilitate or obstruct the various ends which are to be pursued by the mechanism of civil institutions. The state is to have recruits to its strength, and remedies to its distempers. What is the use of discussing a man's abstract right to food or medicine? The question is upon the method of procuring and administering them. In that deliberation I shall always advise to call in the aid of the farmer and the physician rather than the professor of metaphysics.

The science of constructing a commonwealth, or renovating it, or reforming it, is, like every other experimental science, not to be taught a priori. Nor is it a short experience that can instruct us in that practical science, because the real effects of moral causes are not always immediate; but that which in the first instance is prejudicial may be excellent in its remoter operation, and its excellence may arise even from the ill effects it produces in the beginning. The reverse also happens: and very plausible schemes, with very pleasing commencements, have often shameful and lamentable conclusions. In states there are often some obscure and almost latent causes, things which appear at first view of little moment, on which a very great part of its prosperity or adversity may most essentially depend. The science of government being therefore so practical in itself and intended for such practical purposes — a matter which requires experience, and even more experience than any person can gain in his whole life, however sagacious and observing he may be — it is with infinite caution that any man ought to venture upon pulling down an edifice which has answered in any tolerable degree for ages the common purposes of society, or on building it up again without having models and patterns of approved utility before his eyes.

These metaphysic rights entering into common life, like rays of light which pierce into a dense medium, are by the laws of nature refracted from their straight line. Indeed, in the gross and complicated mass of human passions and concerns the primitive rights of men undergo such a variety of refractions and reflections that it becomes absurd to talk of them as if they continued in the simplicity of their original direction. The nature of man is intricate; the objects of society are of the greatest possible complexity; and, therefore, no simple disposition or direction of power can be suitable either to man's nature or to the quality of his affairs. When I hear the simplicity of contrivance aimed at and boasted of in any new political constitutions, I am at no loss to decide that the artificers are grossly ignorant of their trade or totally negligent of their duty. The simple governments are fundamentally defective, to say no worse of them. If you were to contemplate society in but one point of view, all these simple modes of polity are infinitely captivating. In effect each would answer its single end much more perfectly than the more complex is able to attain all its complex purposes. But it is better that the whole should be imperfectly and anomalously answered than that, while some parts are provided for with great exactness, others might be totally neglected or perhaps materially injured by the over-care of a favorite member.

The pretended rights of these theorists are all extremes; and in proportion as they are metaphysically true, they are morally and politically false. The rights of men are in a sort of middle, incapable of definition, but not impossible to be discerned. The rights of men in governments are their advantages; and these are often in balances between differences of good, in compromises sometimes between good and evil, and sometimes between evil and evil. Political reason is a computing principle: adding, subtracting, multiplying, and dividing, morally and not metaphysically or mathematically, true moral denominations.

By these theorists the right of the people is almost always sophistically confounded with their power. The body of the community, whenever it can come to act, can meet with no effectual resistance; but till power and right are the same, the whole body of them has no right inconsistent with virtue, and the first of all virtues, prudence. Men have no right to what is not reasonable and to what is not for their benefit; for though a pleasant writer said, liceat perire poetis, when one of them, in cold blood, is said to have leaped into the flames of a volcanic revolution, ardentem frigidus Aetnam insiluit, I consider such a frolic rather as an unjustifiable poetic license than as one of the franchises of Parnassus; and whether he was a poet, or divine, or politician that chose to exercise this kind of right, I think that more wise, because more charitable, thoughts would urge me rather to save the man than to preserve his brazen slippers as the monuments of his folly (68-74).

Bibliography

Althusius, Johannes. *Politica. An Abridged Translation of Politics Methodically Set Forth and Illustrated with Sacred and Profane Examples*, ed. and trans. Frederick S. Carney. Foreword by Daniel J. Elazar. Indianapolis: Liberty Fund, 1995.

Alvarado, Ruben. *A Common Law: The Law of Nations and Western Civilization*. Aalten: Pietas Press, 1999.

Bellomo, Manlio. *The Common Legal Past of Europe 1000-1800*. Trans. Lydia G. Cochrane. Washington, DC: The Catholic University Press of America, 1995.

Berman, Harold. *Law and Revolution: the Formation of the Western Legal Tradition*. Cambridge, MA: Harvard University Press, 1983.

Calabresi, Guido. *A Common Law for the Age of Statutes*. Cambridge, MA: Harvard University Press, 1982.

Chalmers, Thomas. *On Political Economy, In Connexion With the Moral State and Moral Prospects of Society*. Glasgow: William Collins, 1832.

Chalmers, Thomas. *Problems of Poverty: Selections from the Economic and Social Writings of Thomas Chalmers D.D.*, arr. Henry Hunter. London et al.: Thomas Nelson & Sons, n.d.

Commons, John Rogers. *Institutional Economics: Its Place in Political Economy*. New York: Macmillan, 1934.

Corwin, Edward S. *The "Higher Law" Background of American Constitutional Law*. Ithaca: Cornell University Press, 1955.

Dietze, Gottfried. *America's Political Dilemma: From Limited to Unlimited Democracy*. Baltimore: Johns Hopkins University Press, 1968).

Dietze, Gottfried. *In Defense of Property*. Baltimore: Johns Hopkins University Press, 1963.

Dooyeweerd, Herman. *A New Critique of Theoretical Thought: Volume II*. Amsterdam: H.J. Paris, 1955.

Fromm, Erich. "The Present Human Condition." In *The Dogma of Christ and Other Essays on Religion, Psychology and Culture*

.New York: Holt, Rinehart and Winston, 1963.

Gierke, Otto. *Das deutsche Genossenschaftsrecht. Vol. 2: Geschichte des deutschen Körperschaftsbegriffs.* [The German Law of Association; History of the Germanic Concept of the Corporation] Berlin: Weidmannsche Buchhandlung, 1873.

Grotius, Hugo. *De Jure Praedae Commentarius*, I, trans. G.L. Williams. Oxford, 1950.

Grotius, Hugo. *The Rights of War and Peace*, Book I, ed. Richard Tuck, trans. Jean Barbeyrac. Indianapolis: Liberty Fund, 2005.

Haines, Charles Grove. *The Revival of Natural Law Concepts: A Study of the Establishment and of the Interpretation of Limits on Legislatures with special reference to the Development of certain phases of American Constitutional Law.* Cambridge, MA: Harvard University Press, 1930.

Hayek, Friedrich A. *Law, Legislation, and Liberty. Vol. 1: Rules and Order.* Chicago: University of Chicago Press, 1973.

Hayek, Friedrich A. *Law, Legislation, and Liberty. Vol. 2: The Mirage of Social Justice.* Chicago: University of Chicago Press, 1976.

Hayek, Friedrich A. *Law, Legislation, and Liberty. Vol. 3: The Political Order of a Free People.* Chicago: University of Chicago Press, 1979.

Heinsohn, Gunnar. *Der Erschaffung der Götter: Das Opfer als Ursprung der Religion* [The Creation of the Gods: Sacrifice as the Origin of Religion]. Reinbek: Rowohlt, 1997.

Heinsohn, Gunnar, and Otto Steiger. "The Property Theory of Interest and Money," in *What Is Money?* ed. John Smithin. London: Routledge, 2000.

Heinsohn, Gunnar and Otto Steiger. *Eigentum, Zins und Geld: Ungelöste Rätsel der Wirtschaftswissenschaft* [Property, Interest, and Money: Unsolved Mysteries of Economic Science], 5th edition. Marburg: Metropolis Verlag, 2008.

Justinian, Emperor. *Institutes.* Vol. II of *The Civil Law*, translated, edited, etc. by S.P. Scott A.M. Cincinnati: The Central Trust Company, 1932.

Kirk, Russell. *The Conservative Mind: From Burke to Eliot*, 7th revised edition. Chicago and Washington, DC: Regnery Books, 1986 [1953].

Leoni, Bruno. *Freedom and the Law.* Expanded 3rd edition, foreword by Arthur Kemp. Indianapolis: Liberty Fund, 1991.

Levin, Mark. *Liberty and Tyranny: A Conservative Manifesto.* New York: Simon and Schuster, 2009.

Locke, John. *Two Treatises of Government,* in *The Works, vol. 4: Economic Writings and Two Treatises of Government.* 12th edition. London: Rivington, 1824.

Maine, Henry Sumner. *Ancient Law.* London: Murray, 1861.

Malthus, Thomas Robert. *An Essay on the Principle of Population.* London: J. Johnson, 1798.

McIlwain, Charles Howard. *Constitutionalism: Ancient and Modern.* Ithaca NY, et al.: Cornell University Press, 1940.

Mises, Ludwig von. *The Anti-Capitalistic Mentality.* Grove City, PA: Libertarian Press, 1972 [1956].

Noyes, C. Reinold. *The Institution of Property: A Study of the Development, Substance and Arrangement of the System of Property in Modern Anglo-American Law.* New York: Longman, Green, & Co., 1936.

Oakeshott, Michael. *On Human Conduct.* Oxford: Oxford University Press, 1975.

Ortega y Gasset, José. *The Revolt of the Masses: Authorized Translation from the Spanish.* New York: W. W. Norton & Company, Inc., 1932.

Penn, William, "England's Present Interest Considered," in *The Political Writings of William Penn,* ed. Andrew R. Murphy. Indianapolis: Liberty Fund, 2002.

Perry, Richard L. (ed.). *Sources of Our Liberties: Documentary Origins of Individual Liberties in the United States Constitution and Bill of Rights.* Chicago: American Bar Foundation, 1978.

Pollock, Sir Frederick, and Frederick William Maitland. *The History of English Law Before the Time of Edward I,* 2nd edition, vol. I. Cambridge: At the University Press, 1898.

Pound, Roscoe. *Jurisprudence,* vol. 1. St. Paul, MN: West Publishing Co., 1959.

Rushdoony, Rousas John. *This Independent Republic: Studies in the*

Nature and Meaning of American History. Fairfax VA: Thoburn Press, 1978 [1965].

Schoeck, Helmut, *Envy: A Theory of Social Behaviour.* London: Secker & Warburg, 1966

Smith, Adam. *An Inquiry into the Nature and Causes of the Wealth of Nations.* London: Methuen and Co., Ltd., ed. Edwin Cannan, 1904.

Soto, Hernando de. *The Other Path: The Invisible Revolution in the Third World.* New York: Harper & Row, 1989.

Soto, Hernando de. *The Mystery of Capital: Why Capitalism Triumphs in the West and Fails Everywhere Else.* New York: Basic Books, 2000.

Stahl, Friedrich Julius. *Principles of Law.* Translated, edited, and introduced by Ruben Alvarado. Aalten, the Netherlands: WordBridge Publishing, 2007.

Stahl, Friedrich Julius. *Private Law.* Translated, edited, and introduced by Ruben Alvarado. Aalten, the Netherlands: WordBridge Publishing, 2007.

Stahl, Friedrich Julius. *Die Staatslehre und die Principien des Staatsrechts* [The Doctrine of Law and State on the Basis of the Christian World-View]. Tübingen: Mohr, 1856.

Steiger, Otto, ed. *Property Economics.* Marburg: Metropolis Verlag, 2008.

Stoner, James R. *Common Law and Liberal Theory: Coke, Hobbes, and the Origins of American Constitutionalism.* Lawrence: University of Kansas Press, 1994.

Stoner, James R. *Common-Law Liberty: Rethinking American Constitutionalism.* Lawrence: University of Kansas Press, 2003.

Tierney, Brian. *The Idea of Natural Rights: Studies on Natural Rights, Natural Law, and Church Law, 1150-1625.* Grand Rapids, MI: Wm. B. Eerdmans Publishing Co., 2001.

Tuck, Richard. *Philosophy and Government 1572-1651.* Cambridge: Cambridge University Press, 1993.

Tuck, Richard. *Natural Rights Theories: Their Origin and Development.* Cambridge: Cambridge University Press, 1979.

Weber, Max. *Economy and Society: An Outline of Interpretive Sociology.* Berkeley: University of California Press, 1978.

Weston, Corinne C. "England: Ancient Constitution and Common Law," in *The Cambridge History of Political Thought: 1450-1700*, edited by J. H. Burns with the assistance of Mark Goldie. Cambridge: Cambridge University Press, 1991.

Index